Schools of Quality

Schools of Quality

Third Edition

John Jay Bonstingl

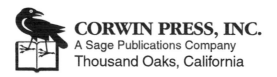

CORWIN PRESS, INC.
A Sage Publications Company
Thousand Oaks, California

For information:

Corwin Press, Inc.
A Sage Publications Company
2455 Teller Road
Thousand Oaks, California 91320
E-mail: order@corwinpress.com

Sage Publications Ltd.
6 Bonhill Street
London EC2A 4PU
United Kingdom

Sage Publications India Pvt. Ltd.
M-32 Market
Greater Kailash I
New Delhi 110 048 India

Printed in the United States of America

Library of Congress Cataloging-in-Publication Data

Bonstingl, John Jay.
    Schools of quality / John Jay Bonstingl.— 3rd ed.
        p.   cm.
    Includes bibliographical references (p.   ).
    ISBN 0-7619-7854-2 (cloth) — ISBN 0-7619-7855-0 (pbk.)
    1. School management and organization—United States. 2. Total quality management—United States. 3. Education—United States—Philosophy.   I. Title.
    LB2805 .B65 2001
    371.2'00973—dc21   2001028210

This book is printed on acid-free paper.

01   02   03   04   05   06   10   9   8   7   6   5   4   3   2   1

Acquisitions Editor:	Rachel Livsey
Corwin Editorial Assistant:	Phyllis Cappello
Production Editor:	Nevair Kabakian
Cover Designer:	Michael Dubowe

Contents

Praise for *Schools of Quality*, Third Edition

"*Jay Bonstingl's book* **Schools of Quality** *is an excellent resource for understanding and developing Quality measures in a school setting. He provides an easy-to-follow framework for implementation. He demonstrates how Quality concepts, once considered only applicable in business and industry, can successfully be utilized to enhance school improvement initiatives. It should be required reading for educators formulating an improvement plan.*"

Edward Bernetich
Principal, Beachwood Middle School,
A Twice-Recognized Blue Ribbon National School of Excellence
Beachwood, Ohio

"*. . .the best introduction to Quality Philosophy available to practitioners today. Bonstingl has skillfully interpreted the Quality philosophy to help create environments where the generation of profound knowledge allows school districts to continuously improve.*"

Leo P. Corriveau, Ph.D.
Superintendent of Schools, SAU #34
Hillsboro, New Hampshire

"*When leaders of education organizations seek to transform their schools into functional systems, they turn to Jay Bonstingl for support and are guided by the principles and practices in* **Schools of Quality.** *Dr. Bonstingl's work should be read by all educators seeking to implement quality practices in their schools.*"

Blanca E. Enriquez
Director
Region 19 Head Start
El Paso, Texas

Bonstingl provides a research-based foundation of quality principles currently used in schools. He captures the creative ideas of many quality practitioners providing inspiration to work through continuous improvement in the classroom."

Karen R. Fauss
Classroom teacher and author of *Continuous Improvement in the Primary Classroom: Language Arts (K-3)*

More praise for *Schools of Quality*, Third Edition, on page 140.

Prologue
The New World of Quality

I t was very late—two minutes before midnight according to the clock on the wall behind the hotel's registration counter. I had just arrived in Dallas after two long connecting flights from Minneapolis, where earlier that day I gave the keynote address at a conference on Quality in Education, followed by a three-hour workshop on Quality-focused interactive classroom strategies and tools for teachers and students. Battling a snow and ice storm on the way to the Minneapolis airport, I nearly missed my flight. With only a breakfast roll and a cup of coffee in the early morning and a bag of peanuts and a coke on the plane, I arrived at the hotel tired and hungry.

"Could you point me toward a restaurant that would be open at this time of night?" I asked the young man behind the counter.

"Well, our restaurant is closed for the evening," he said, shrugging his shoulders. "And I notice you don't have a car. I'm sorry, but there's nothing open within walking distance. What are you hungry for?"

My mouth watered as I envisioned the possibilities. "Let's see. Chicken salad on rye with lettuce and tomato, a diet cola with a lemon wedge," I replied, "and maybe a few potato chips on the side," knowing full well that it would be morning before I'd be able to have anything to eat.

"Fine, sir! I'll take care of it!" the young man proclaimed with a big grin. "You go on up to your room and I'll make it for you myself."

I'm sure the astonishment must have shown on my face. "Should I call room service?" I asked.

"No sir. Just leave it up to me. I'll have it delivered to your room in about fifteen minutes."

I barely had time to unpack when there was a knock at my door. A young woman dressed in a black suit and tie, carrying a heavy round serving tray, asked permission to come into the room. On the tray, to my great delight, was a rye sandwich piled high with chicken salad, fresh potato chips, three ripe and juicy strawberries, and a glass of ice-cold cola with a lemon wedge!

"This is wonderful. You have no idea how much I appreciate this!" I exclaimed. "How much do I owe you?" I asked, as I dug into my pockets.

"Not a thing," the young woman replied with a smile. "It's on the house."

This was certainly far more than I had expected, especially so late at night. "Well," I responded, "at least let me give you a nice tip."

"Oh, no sir," she declined. "I couldn't take a tip."

"Really? Why not," I inquired.

"Because I'm the manager of the hotel!"

In less than a half hour, she and her thoughtful and energetic front desk clerk had made me a lifelong fan of their hotel. They both took the time and effort to build a relationship with me, even though I would be in their hotel for only a few hours.

Today, world-class business leaders throughout the United States and around our planet are becoming more and more aware that their own success depends upon their ability to create good relationships. When employees know that their boss truly cares about them, they are more likely to put their hearts and souls into their work, which creates the impetus for them, in turn, to delight their customers.

When people know that you genuinely have their best interest at heart, they make you their choice. When you work to make others successful and happy, their success will make you successful in return.

Companies who understand this basic truth will survive and thrive in the twenty-first-century economy. Those businesses that are not focused on helping people to succeed may, in time, find that they have no loyal customers, no enthusiastic employees, and no future.

This is the harsh and uncompromising reality of modern-day business in the highly competitive Quality-focused global economy.

This is also the reality of our schools and school systems. Our parents and taxpayers will continue to support our work in public education to the extent they are convinced that we are helping all students and their families to succeed.

We know that people most often fail when they are without meaningful relationships, or when their relationships cause them to feel unwanted, misunderstood, or stupid. People succeed best when their relationships are strong, supportive, and loving. Our relationship systems are the most important factors determining our levels of satisfaction at home, at work, and in our communities. The quality of our relationships determines the quality of our lives.

Similarly, the quality of relationships inside the schoolhouse determines, in large measure, the quality of the work done by the students, teachers, administrators, and support staff. When I enter a school for the first time, it usually takes no more than a few minutes to discern whether this is a place of loving support, creative encouragement, and safety from physical and emotional harm. The school's climate may not be visible to the eye, but it is often so palpable that it seems you could actually cut it with a knife.

Now, more than ever before, the central role of Quality in our schools is crucial to our success, and especially to the success of our students. Our public schools are under constant fire from the media, from politicians, and from those in our society who (for their own reasons) would like to see public education evaporate into thin air. Public education in America will live into the future only if our efforts, and the results of those efforts, are perceived to be high quality. The question is: Can we—*will we*—rise to the challenge?

Since the publication of the first edition of *Schools of Quality* in the early 1990s, thousands of schools and school systems throughout North America and around the world have invested in their own Quality journeys, and they have seen remarkable results. Quality has become more than just an idea, more than a slogan. In those schools where Quality is taken seriously, Quality has become a way of life for everyone. It is "just the way we do things around here."

Administrators in what I call "Schools of Quality" report that their relationships with their colleagues and staff have become less adversarial, more collaborative; less suspicious, more trusting; less fear-filled, more creative and supportive. Relations between school boards and central office administration are smoother, with a greater appreciation on both sides of the need for collaboration. Boards create policies that are best for the schools and the community; central office leadership works closely with the board to build a culture of Quality in which everyone can succeed and take pride and joy in their work together. Similarly, relations between administration and teacher organizations become more mutually supportive and trusting as they work together as full partners in the progress of the community's children and families.

Teachers in Schools of Quality report similar changes. They no longer dread classroom observations because they use these occasions to improve upon the good work they are already doing. In the faculty lounge and teacher's lunchroom, instead of backbiting and negativity, teachers engage in conversations that make everyone feel that he or she is an important part of the school community, with unique contributions to make for the common good. Discussions focus not on what's wrong and who's to blame, but rather on practical, constructive ways to improve upon current successes for the benefit of all.

Teachers in Schools of Quality view themselves more as a "guide on the side" than as a "sage on the stage." They consciously work to create environments that challenge their students to develop their potential to the fullest. They use a variety of assessment types, including tests, portfolios, demonstrations of mastery, research projects, and other opportunities to help students discover how much they have learned and how much they have yet to master. These teachers know that teaching young people *how* to learn is as important as teaching them *what* to learn.

Students enjoy coming to school when teachers focus on ways of enabling every student to succeed. Students get more involved in their work, not only for the grade, but for the intrinsic satisfaction they get from doing good work and building new competencies upon what they already do well. In Schools of Quality, students learn how to work productively alone and in teams, how to assess the quality of their work, and how to improve their processes of critical and creative thinking, studying, and learning. School becomes an exploration, a journey of discovery, with their teachers as guides and mentors helping them toward greater and greater success.

Parents are avid supporters of Schools of Quality because they see the positive differences in their children's spirit for learning. Young people in such environments take greater responsibility for their own learning and for their own lives. They learn to use time more efficiently. They learn how to solve problems more creatively. They begin to understand and apply the Quality principles that will one day bring them successes in their chosen professions, in their roles as parents and as active, responsible participants in our democratic experiment. They will also find that the Quality way of life makes a positive difference in their experience of life—mentally, physically, emotionally, and spiritually.

Business and civic leaders are eager to support the Quality focus of the community's schools. High-quality citizens and workers come from Schools of Quality. Many enlightened business leaders encourage their schools to participate in Quality-focused programs such as the U.S. Department of Education's Blue Ribbon Schools program and the Malcolm Baldrige National Quality Program, not necessarily to win an award but rather to engage in a nationally recognized process of self-assessment and continuous improvement. Those schools and districts who are dedicated to an ongoing Quality journey may also apply for participation in the Comprehensive School Quality Audit conducted by The Center for Schools of Quality, a unique opportunity to identify current strengths and to recognize areas for potential improvement in all facets and at all levels of the organization.

If you are new to this book, let me take you on a brief tour. My reason for writing *Schools of Quality* is to give educators and their stakeholders a practical, useful set of tools and knowledge, so they are able to understand the basic ideas of the Quality Philosophy and to put these ideas to work in their schools as well as in their own personal and professional lives.

In Chapter 1, "The Bell Curve Meets *Kaizen*," we take a look at one of the fundamental ideas of the Quality Philosophy. People tend to build their futures upon what they understand of their past. The bell curve limits success to a few students, while others become reinforced in their self-concept of mediocrity and failure. Systems (including schools and classes) work best when the system is set up in such a way that everyone learns how to succeed.

Chapter 2, "Quality Comes (Back) to America," explores the history of the Quality movement and the early pioneers who helped Japan rise from the ashes of World War II to become one of the economic superpowers of the world. The advice Deming and his fellow Quality proponents gave to Japan and later to American business leaders, is equally applicable to our world of education. The solutions to many of our problems lie in our ability to look carefully at the cultural contexts in which we work and live.

In Chapter 3, "Learning a New Way to Swim," we examine our American culture and the presumptions we make every day about the way things are and the way things are supposed to be. Our ways of thinking about ourselves and our beliefs seem to us as "right" and natural as the watery environment seems to a fish. As we look more closely at our surrounding culture, we discover some of the hidden reasons for our current dilemmas.

Chapter 4, "Reconsidering the Better Mousetrap," poses a question: Is it more beneficial to invent a better mousetrap, or to find a way to discourage mice from coming to your home in the first place? How could we improve the quality of our schools by creating the circumstances for success, rather than inspecting-out that which goes wrong? We look at what I call the Four Pillars of Quality and see how they can be useful in building a "mouse-free" environment in which all students learn and succeed.

"Defining the Real Business of Schools of Quality" is the focus of Chapter 5. The most successful businesses ask themselves three essential questions to guide their improvement. So should we in the field of education: What business are we really in? What do we mean by success? How can we achieve greater and greater success for everyone?

Chapter 6, "Continuing the Journey," will give you a collection of tried-and-true practical tips and strategies to make your Quality journey successful for you and everyone in your sphere of influence.

Finally, Chapter 7 is all about "Quality as a Way of Life." How can each of us benefit personally from making Quality the way we live our lives? I offer five personal practices of Quality to enrich your life at home, at work, in the community, and in your life of the spirit.

There are eight appendices. Appendix 1, "Tools for the Transformation," gives you a set of tools to use in the classroom, in planning districtwide Quality initiatives, and to improve your everyday functioning. Examples of school-based uses are given for each tool.

Appendix 2, "The Four Pillars of Schools of Quality," is a chart showing the possible contributions of policy-makers, school leaders, teachers, students, parents and families, business people, and community members in making the school's Quality journey success-filled for all stakeholders.

Appendix 3, "Deming's Fourteen Points Applied to Companies and Schools," offers a three-column chart showing how the basic ideas of one of Quality's early pioneers can relate to the work of both schools and businesses. Here is a common language that will help educators and business people to understand the other's world, so they can combine efforts more easily.

Appendix 4, "The Quality Paradigm Shift in Education," provides in chart form a comparison between the old paradigm of teaching testing and the new Quality-focused paradigm of continuous learning and improvement. We all know that testing for the sake of testing is futile. Here's why.

Appendix 5, "The Educational Impact of the Quality Philosophy in Schools," is a summary of the findings of The Conference Board of Canada, stemming from their extensive study of Quality in education in the early 1990s. Their discoveries are as applicable today as they were then.

Appendix 6, "The SCANS Report," will give you the executive summary of this landmark document describing five essential competencies and a three-part foundation that all young people will need to have in order to survive and thrive in a Quality-focused global economy.

Appendix 7, "The Malcolm Baldrige National Quality Program," explores the core values and concepts, as well as the seven main criteria of the Malcolm Baldrige program in education. There are many statewide variations on this national program.

Appendix 8, "Sources of Additional Information," gives you an extensive bibliography of books, articles, and organizations for further information on the philosophy and practice of Quality.

My thanks to all of our readers who told us what you liked in the first and second editions of *Schools of Quality*, and for all of your suggestions, many of which we have incorporated into this new third edition.

My very best wishes go with you as you embark on, or continue, your personal and organizational Quality journey. Bon voyage!

John Jay Bonstingl
Columbia, Maryland
March 2001

Acknowledgments

I am indebted to a great many people for helping me think through the concepts of TQM and supporting my efforts in a wide variety of ways. My appreciation, first and foremost, to the late W. Edwards Deming for his pioneering work in this field, and for taking time to share his invaluable insights with me. My appreciation also to Ceil Kilian, his longtime assistant, for her many kindnesses.

My appreciation also goes to: David Bayless, Nancy Bayless, and Gabriel Massaro, Bayless & Associates; The Reverend Barclay Brown; Michael J. Clark, independent journalist; Clare Crawford-Mason, Robert Mason, and Scott Stein, CC-M Productions; Lorraine Flowers, Maryland State Department of Education; Barry Gomberg, Weber State College; Anne Gurvin, U.S. Information Agency; Julie Horine, University of Mississippi; Barara Hummell, Madison Area Quality Improvement Network; Linda James, former education specialist for the Malcolm Baldrige National Quality Award; Ed Janus, Corporate Radio Network; Don McCain, World Center for Community Excellence; former Texas Governor Ann Richards; Jay McTighe, Maryland Assessment Consortium; Carl Marburger and Barbara Hansen, consultants in school-community relations; Tom Mosgaller, City of Madison Wisconsin; Jan Partain, Arkansas Industrial Development Committee; Yvonne Thayer, Virginia State Department of Education; Marshall Sashkin, OERI, U.S. Department of Education; Karen Schriver, Carnegie Mellon University; Peggy Siegel, Sandra Byrne, Patricia Mitchell, National Alliance of Business; Ronald Pahl, California State University, Fullerton; Lewis Rhodes, Martha Bozman, and Judy Nash, formerly of AASA's Quality Network; Pam Sheehan, World Affairs Council of Pittsburgh; Fred Shemanek, North Central Deming Management Forum; Jim Sheridan, The Olive Branch Restaurant; and Jeaette Stanko, University of Maryland, Baltimore County.

Thanks also to my international friends and colleagues for their bountiful assistance: Hon. Shinichiro Horie, Embassy of Japan; Professor Shinichi Suzuki, Waseda University, Tokyo; Junji Noguchi, Japanese Union of Scientists and Engineers; Professor Jost Reischmann, University of Tübingen, Germany; Professor Shi Weiping, East China Normal University; László Arató, Hungarian Institute of Public Education; Professors Beáta Kochy and Ivan Falus of Eötvös Loránd University, Budapest, Hungary; Michael Carruthers, South African Quality Institute; and Professors Unni Hagen and Ellen Carm, University of Oslo, Norway.

My thanks to the school leaders who shared ideas and insights on TQM with me over the years: Kenneth Arndt, Elyria, Ohio; Patrick Konopnicki and Diane Barker, Virginia Beach, Virginia; Spicer Bell, Cambridge, Maryland; Den Boyd, Prince William County, Virginia; Robert Bender, Meadville, Pennsylvania; Albertha Caldwell, Glenwood, Maryland; Phyllis Cohen, Nelson Diaz, Merri Mann, and Janet McAliley, Miami, Florida; Robert D. Conn, Holden, Massachusetts; Thomas Conner, Washington, Pennsylvania; Bonnie Daniel, Columbia, Maryland; David Gangel, Rappahannock County, Virginia; Constance Goldman, Cape Elizabeth, Maine; Debby Estes, Sherman, Texas, Robert Gratz, Belvidere, New Jersey; Terry Grier, Akron Ohio; Thomas Houlihan, Johnston County, North Carolina; Lee Jenkins, Redding, California; Christine Jensen, Anchorage, Alaska; Thomas Labanc, Upper St. Clair, Pennsylvania; Paul Longhofer, Wichita, Kansas; Larry Macaluso, Red Lion, Pennsylvania; Charles Melvin, Beloit-Turner, Wisconsin; Harrell G. Miller, Napa, California; Randee Reisinger, Waco, Texas; Larrae Rocheleau, Sitka, Alaska; Charles Slemenda, Tarboro, North Carolina; Len Strnad, Elyria, Ohio; Franklin Schargel, Brooklyn, New York; Richard Ten Haken, Spencerport, New York; Guy Vander Vliet, Piscataway, New Jersey; John Vanko, St. Charles, Illinois; Thomas E. Walsh, Casper, Wyoming; and Richard Weeter, Oklahoma City, Oklahoma.

I would also like to express my thanks to Paul Houston of AASA; Leo Corriveau, SAU #34 in New Hampshire; Mick McNiel of AASA Quality Network and the Woods Quality Center in Iowa; Paul Williams and Ed Bernetich, Beachwood Public Schools in Ohio; Blanca E. Enriquez, Region 19 Head Start in El Paso; Celso Leite of Fundaçao Limeira in Brazil; Hayal Köksal, cofounder of the Turkish Center for Schools of Quality; Judy Krohn, Texas Education Agency; Richard Christensen, Karen R. Fauss, Shelly Carson, and Jeff Burgard of Enterprise School District in California; Hal and Marcia Wilson of Walnut Creek, California; and Anthony Scannella of the Foundation for Educational Administration; Robert Wilson, Keystone Training & Consulting, Pittsburgh; Dean Hubbard, Max Ruhl, and John Jasinski of Northwest Missouri State University; Stan Slessor and Jim Jenssen, Waverly-Shell Rock Schools in Iowa; Doug Long, Bob Wilhite, Greg Wojcik, and Joan McGarry of District 215 in Illinois; Mihail Mehesh, Uzhgorod, Ukraine; Brenda Wright, French Polynesia; and Richard Hayward and At Meyer, leaders of the Quality education movement in South Africa. A world of thanks to Linda James for her enduring support and advice, and to Ron Brandt and Nancy Modrak for their abiding faith in the first incarnations of this work.

My special appreciation to Louise Voss Thurn, Keystone Area Education Agency, for her unique insights and constant support. Special thanks also to my longtime assistant Stephanie Steinert for quality service well beyond the call of duty. And my eternal gratitude to Gracia Alkema of Corwin Press for believing in the value of my work and giving me the unique opportunity of sharing my ideas with educational leaders and innovators around the world through this book.

There are many others whose significant contributions are not recognized here due to the failure of memory, and I beg their forgiveness. Please know that their ideas have helped greatly.

Of course, all of the ideas expressed here are ultimately my sole responsibility, and they should not be construed as reflecting the beliefs of the many people who helped bring this book to fruition.

J.J.B.

About the Author

John Jay Bonstingl has been a classroom teacher; textbook author; host of TV and radio news and current affairs programs; producer of educational videos for the classroom; a popular and sought-after keynote speaker for business, education, and organizational conferences throughout North America and overseas; consultant to corporations, governments, nonprofit organizations, and school systems around the world; and advisor to more than twenty ministries of education worldwide. His work has been featured on television and radio worldwide, including C-SPAN, CNN, and "Good Morning South Africa."

Mr. Bonstingl has helped communities and a wide range of organizations, including businesses, schools and colleges, Head Start, and school-to-career programs, to adopt Quality concepts as their philosophical and operational foundation. As founder and president of Bonstingl Leadership Development and its education outreach organization, The Center for Schools of Quality, Mr. Bonstingl and his team provide effective consultation and training in the application of Quality principles and practices. He has served as an examiner for the Malcolm Baldrige National Quality Award, and as a judge for the U.S. Department of Education's Blue Ribbon Schools Program. He and his team conduct an extensive Comprehensive School Quality Audit for schools and districts who are committed to continual improvement through Quality principles and practices. Mr. Bonstingl is also available to give on-site workshops and private consultation for schools' business partners and civic organizations who want to learn how to improve their own functioning and productivity.

BONSTINGL LEADERSHIP DEVELOPMENT
The Center for Schools of Quality
Post Office Box 810
Columbia, Maryland 21044 USA
Telephone: (410) 997-7555
24-Hour Fax: (410) 997-2345
Direct E-Mail: Bonstingl@aol.com

*Dedicated to the loving memory of my
Father, Mother, and Aunt Madeline, who gave me
my earliest and most important lessons in Quality.*

1

The Bell Curve Meets *Kaizen*

ot long ago, I conducted an inservice seminar for teachers who were using a textbook I had authored. One of the teachers stayed behind to talk with me after the seminar. His red coach's jacket was inscribed with the name "Bob."

"Jay," he began solemnly, "I want to tell you something about your book."

"Please tell me," I responded.

"Well, I've really enjoyed teaching with it. The kids love it, too, and I get high marks from their parents. But I'm having one big problem with that textbook of yours." Bob showed a hint of a smile.

"Really? Tell me about it," I replied.

His expression became stern again.

"In the four years I've used your book for my course, none of my students has ever made lower than a B, and I don't give away grades."

I'm sure my face showed my delight.

"Well, congratulations, Bob! That's quite a success story. All of your students are succeeding in the learning process, and they're enjoying it! That's terrific! You must be very proud!"

He shook his head slowly. I was baffled.

"So, Bob, what's the problem?"

"My kids are all getting high grades, and they're all enjoying the course. *That's the problem!* My administrators think my course is worthless unless a sizeable percentage of my students are making C's, D's, and failing grades! I guess we're *too* successful!"

Bob then took out some of his students' work to assure me that his standards were very high. It was some of the best student work I had ever seen, demonstrating a variety of fresh perspectives expressed with creativity, self-confidence, and enthusiasm.

"This is great stuff!" I exclaimed.

Bob sighed and looked away, a flash of anger crossing his face. "None of that work deserves a C," he said, "and certainly not anything lower."

I agreed.

"Bob, is this what we're really talking about?" I picked up a piece of chalk and drew a bell-shaped curve on the board.

Bob nodded. "That's it! My administrators think that a bell curve is the ideal result of good work. Dumb, isn't it?"

Dumb, maybe. But this conception of educational success has been around for a long time. I thought about all the times I had heard teachers and administrators from every region of the country refer to this philosophy. In fact, the bell curve was a fundamental tenet of the education courses I took in college, modeled by my cooperating teacher in the student teaching experience, and confirmed by standard practice thereafter in every secondary school in which I taught.

I thought of the contrasting views of success I have heard over the years from elementary and high school teachers who participated in the graduate education classes I teach.

I always enjoy asking them this question: "How do you know when you're successful in your teaching?" Almost invariably, elementary school teachers tell me that they know they are most successful when their students are all continuously improving and feeling good about themselves and their new learnings.

What a contrast with the answer many high school teachers give to the same question! "My course has real meat to it," one Advanced Placement history teacher beamed. "Very few students have ever gotten an *A* in *my* class!"

A college professor I had in a seminar for German majors had put it similarly many years ago as he explained his grading policy on the first day of class: "*A*'s are for *Gott*," he declared, pointing to the heavens. "*B*'s are for scholars such as myself," he proclaimed with an open hand pointing at his chest. He paused for a deep breath. "*C*'s, *D*'s, and *E*'s are for you," he said with his right arm sweeping across the classroom, as he consigned all of us to the depths of mediocrity and worse.

Why does it seem that the farther we get from 1st grade, the less likely we are to view education's central purpose as nurturing people's innate potential through the development of patterns of success, and the more likely we are to view education as a judgmental, gatekeeping function?

Bob's voice broke my reverie. "Jay, what can I tell my administrators so they understand where I'm coming from?"

I thought for a moment. Bob's coach's jacket provided me with an insight.

"You're a football coach, right?"

He nodded.

"Okay, take a look at this line of scrimmage." I drew this figure on the board:

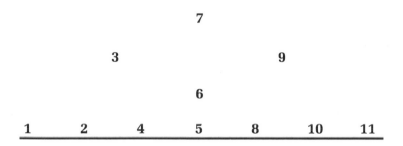

"If we were to create a bell curve for your team," I suggested, "might it look like this?" I continued my drawing, superimposing a bell curve over the players' positions.

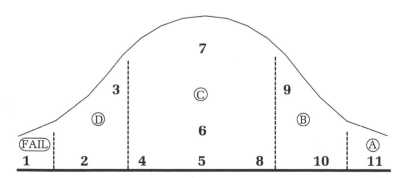

"Okay, let's say player #11 is terrific—a real all-star." He does everything right. Player #1, on the other hand, has absolutely no understanding of the game. He can't even move. His feet might as well be cemented to the ground."

Bob offered to continue my metaphor: "Players #2 and #3 aren't much better, but players #9 and #10 are very good—not as good as #11, but still very good."

"Players #4, #5, #6, #7, and #8," Bob continued, "are only average. And just look at the positions they are playing—the most important positions on the team!"

Bob stopped to think about what he had just said. "No, actually that's not right. *Each* of those positions is important. The team works like a system. If all of the system's parts are working together successfully, we do well. But if any part of the system shows any weakness, you can bet the opposing team will capitalize on it."

"Okay, Coach," I said, pointing to the bell-curved football team on the board, "what kind of a season do you think this team is going to have?"

Bob chuckled. "I wouldn't want to coach that team, Jay. It's going to be a long season for them!"

Bob then shared one of his "success secrets" with me. "When things are really clicking in my classroom, it's a lot like a championship football team playing on the field. There's a kind of electricity in the air. Everybody is psyched up and they are all helping each other, making sure that everybody on the team is successful. There's a special *synergy*—everybody feeding on one another's enthusiasm and dedication and sharp focus. It's an amazing sight!"

Bob thought silently for a moment, then said, "Why can't our schools be like that?"

Why, indeed!

I shared with Bob another analogy. "What might happen if, today, all the chief executive officers of all the businesses in the United States—from Exxon and General Motors down to the smallest mom-and-pop stores—sat down at one huge conference table and agreed that from this day forward they would all, *by design*, make sure that every day's products and services conform to the bell-shaped curve? Some of their output would be good or even excellent, but most would be mediocre or inferior. How long would such businesses survive in today's highly competitive global marketplace?"

"But," Bob retorted, "even the harshest critics of American education wouldn't suggest that we deliberately design mediocrity and failure into the work we do with kids in schools, would they?"

Maybe not. But ask children who have been in school for a few years, and you will find that almost all of them know in which of the five pigeonholes of the bell curve they "belong." One bright 4th grade girl once told me, with a weary voice, that she never was good in math and that she would probably always get low grades in that subject. Early academic failures tend to be self-fulfilling prophesies for later years. Young people who grow up believing that they are incapable of achieving quality results in their schoolwork, despite their best efforts, begin to see *themselves* as having little inherent quality. Rightly or wrongly, they may even come to believe that schools exist not to help them improve, but rather to judge, criticize, and rank-order their efforts.

Today, a philosophy called Total Quality and its practice, called Total Quality Management (TQM), are helping educators view themselves as supporters rather than judges, as mentors and coaches rather than lecturers, as partners with parents, students, administrators, teachers, businesses, and entire communities rather than isolated workers within the walls of the classroom. We now understand that the only way we can ensure our own growth is by helping others to grow; the only way to maximize our own potentials is by helping others to improve little by little, day by day. The Japanese call this personal dedication to mutual improvement *kaizen*. The deeply ingrained ethos of *kaizen* lies at the heart of Japan's miraculous postwar revival. It is also the heart and soul of Total Quality. In this book we explore the new world of TQM, from its American origins in this century to its abrogation by American industry and its adoption (through the efforts of American statistical consultants) by major Japanese industries and Japanese society.

Thousands of schools and communities are now beginning to explore ways of adopting Total Quality as an operational norm. The people of these schools and communities are in the process of transforming their thoughts and lifestyles to mirror the crucial decision they have made to dedicate their efforts to continuous self-improvement and to the continuous improvement of the people with whom they live, work, and study.

The principles and practices of Total Quality Management have much to teach educators, as we join in the struggle to transform our entire society from a "Nation at Risk" into a Nation of Quality.

2

Quality Comes (Back) to America

Remember when the words "Made in Japan" were the cause of laughter, scorn, and derision? Before and shortly after World War II, Japanese products were widely regarded—and with good reason—as cheap, poorly made, and easily destructible. On his television show, Jack Benny poked fun at Japanese manufacturing quality by wearing an inexpensive, new "Japanese" suit that came apart, piece by piece, during his monologue. The audience roared with laughter, acknowledging the essential truth not only of Benny's vaunted frugality, but also of the widely held public perception of Japanese goods.

Modern-day Japan, by contrast, is one of the world's great economic and industrial powers. "Made in Japan" is now considered the emblem of highest quality in virtually every type of item Japan exports. Japanese industrial and government leaders credit Japan's dramatic postwar turnaround in great part to a small group of Americans, including W. Edwards Deming and Joseph M. Juran, who taught Japanese industrialists the principles of statistical process control (SPC), a methodology for consistently producing high-quality goods and services.

Today, the watchword of successful persons, businesses, schools, and other organizations worldwide is "Quality." Our understanding of Total Quality and its implications for education will depend upon an understanding of TQM's development in the United States and the Americans who developed it.

The Beginning of the Total Quality Concept

William Edwards Deming was born on October 14, 1900,* and earned his Ph.D. in physics at Yale in 1927. As a graduate student in the late 1920s, Deming worked summer jobs in Chicago at Western Electric's Hawthorne plant, the site of later experiments by Harvard researcher Elton Mayo on the correlations between the work environment, employee motivation, and productivity.

At Hawthorne, Deming observed the sweatshop conditions under which the predominantly female workforce of 46,000 labored to produce telephone equipment. The Hawthorne plant, like many other production facilities in the industrialized world of the early 20th century, operated under the philosophy of "scientific management" popularized by Frederick Winslow Taylor, an American industrial engineer. Taylor taught industrialists that workers should be hired to perform a small number of tasks in a repetitive, mechanistic fashion. They should not be hired to think about the work they do because thinking was the rightful role of management. Factory owners, according to Taylor, were to plan the work process and hire managers who would direct the workers. Workers, largely uneducated and untrained for the job, were urged by their bosses to continuously "work harder" and "do their best."

Scientific management principles discouraged workers from considering ways they could work more effectively and efficiently. Workers would surely make mistakes, but the inspectors at the end of the production line could catch faulty products before they left the plant, and workers' per-piece pay could be lowered for each item that had to be scrapped or reworked. If a worker produced too many faulty items, he or she could be dismissed.

Taylor's scientific management philosophy viewed the entire production process mechanistically. Equipment was designed to be interchangeable and easily replaceable, and workers were thought about in similar terms. Taylor taught American industry to view every line worker as "a cog in the giant industrial machine, whose job could be defined and directed by appropriately educated managers, administering a set of rules" (Walton 1991). Tasks on the assembly line were simple, repetitive, and boring. Workers' compliance with management's dictates was ensured by the hierarchical, top-down paradigm reminiscent of the turn-

---

*W. Edwards Deming was 93 years old at the time of his death.

of-the-century Prussian army. In line with Taylor's model, workers at the Hawthorne plant were paid according to the number of pieces they produced per day. Higher output meant higher take-home pay. Quality of work was not a consideration for most workers. Inspectors at the end of the production line were entrusted with quality control, to the extent that product quality was an issue.

This philosophy of management was well-suited to the assembly-line processes developed by Henry Ford and copied widely in America's private and public sectors. Taylor's philosophy made it possible for waves of immigrants, many of whom could not read, write, speak English, or oftentimes even communicate with one another, to find employment in American factories. Taylor's ideas soon found their way into the nation's schools. The turn-of-the-century mass education movement took as its model the American factory, complete with the philosophy of scientific management. Franklin Bobbitt of the University of Chicago "took on the role of translating Frederick Taylor's principles . . . into a form in which they could be used by educators." He, like Taylor, believed that

> efficiency depended on the 'centralization of authority and definite direction by the supervisors of all processes performed . . . . The worker [that is, the teacher] . . . must be kept supplied with the detailed instructions as to the work to be done, the standards to be reached, the methods to be employed, and the appliances to be used . . . .' The results of the work of the planning department had to be 'transmitted to the teachers so that there can never be any misunderstanding as to what is expected of a teacher in the way of results or in the matter of method. This means that instruction must be given as to everything that is to be done' (Callahan from Marshall and Tucker 1992).

At the Hawthorne Plant, Deming became convinced that the authoritarian Taylor method of management was degrading to the human spirit and counterproductive to the interests of employees, management, and the company.

At Bell Laboratories in New Jersey, Deming met Walter A. Shewhart, a statistician who was leading the company's efforts to improve the reliability of telephones. Shewhart's goal was to make phones so well that the American phrase "as alike as two peas" would be replaced by "as alike as two telephones" (Kilian 1992). Toward this goal, Shewhart developed a methodology for improving worker performance and production output by measuring the extent to which the items produced fell within acceptable limits of variation. Shewhart developed a way of showing this variation graphically, which he called a statistical control chart. He shared his findings with Deming, his young protégé.

Deming recognized that, with training, workers could keep control charts of their own work and thus monitor the quality of the items they sent down the production line. Deming believed that if workers could be educated and empowered to manage their own work processes, the quality of their output would improve and the costly and ineffective end-of-line inspection process could be curtailed or eliminated. High quality would cost less, not more.

Shewhart also showed Deming a three-step cyclical process to help ensure increasingly higher quality production. Shewhart's cycle of Specification-Production-Inspection focused attention on inspection as the genesis of revised specifications, rather than as an end-of-line failsafe mechanism.

Deming later modified this three-step cycle into a four-step process, now commonly known as the Deming Cycle or the PDSA Cycle (although Deming always referred to it as the Shewhart Cycle in honor of his mentor).

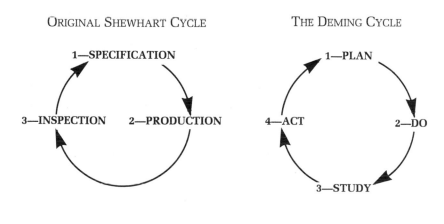

ORIGINAL SHEWHART CYCLE   THE DEMING CYCLE

The Deming Cycle (Plan-Do-Study-Act)[1], like Shewhart's earlier model, is cyclical: First, a production plan is created. Then the plan is implemented on a small scale. In the third stage, production is studied to make sure it conforms to the plan. Finally, lessons learned in the study stage are used to modify the ongoing production process so that a new set of data can be used in creating and implementing the next plan, on a larger scale. Thus, the PDSA Cycle is a simple, effective, data-driven instrument for continuous learning and improvement.

Shewhart's discoveries and teachings became the centerpiece of Deming's emerging philosophy of Quality Management, which he taught first to Americans, then to the vanquished Japanese. During World War II, Deming was called by the U.S. government to support the war effort. As David Halberstam recounts, the War Department, impressed by Shewhart's work, brought together a small group of experts on statistical process control to help establish quality guidelines for defense contractors. Deming was part of that group, and he "came to love the work, for it concerned itself not just with mathematical excellence but with social value as well, helping people to make their products better and thus to make lives better" (Halberstam 1986).

Using Deming's application of Shewhart's ideas in the war effort, American manufacturers were able to produce superior military equipment. Japanese engineers studying captured American planes realized by 1942 that Japan's military fortunes were doomed.

> As they examined captured material they were sickeningly aware that the Americans were turning out better-made machines—machines that were obviously mass-produced— and that Japanese pilots were being sent into the skies hopelessly mismatched. Even in the postwar years, the Japanese were embarrassed by the shoddiness of their goods. If it rained in Tokyo, ten thousand phones might be out of order (Halberstam 1986).

At the war's end, American industry converted to peacetime production of goods and services for a voracious, affluent American public and worked to satisfy consumers' material needs and wants worldwide. As beneficiaries of the only industrialized economy left unscathed by the war, American industry could hardly keep up with demand. In the

---

[1]Deming's PDSA Cycle was originally known as the PDCA Cycle, with "check" in place of "study."

rush to satisfy consumer demand, American manufacturers focused on increasing production, leaving behind the quest for ever-increasing quality. Deming's frustration grew. He saw mounting evidence of America's abandonment of his and Shewhart's work. "Nothing was left of it, not even dust," said Deming (Deming seminar 1992).

And yet, in the late 1940s, many American manufacturers boasted about the quality built into their products. Companies such as Ford spoke with pride about the personal attention their workers gave to every aspect of production. *The Quality Revolution* (1989) shows a clip of a 1949 promotional film with a family climbing into their new Ford convertible at a dealer's showroom and driving home, as the announcer's voice says of the new owners: "As the road unfolds under their air-cushioned wheels, they are not quite alone." Each car carries "something of the designers who took ideas and put them on paper, something of the tool-and-die men, the core makers, the girls who lubricated the steel sheets when they went into the press. The skills, the heart they put into their work rides with this car always!"

Ironically, over the next 30 years, the decline of the American car industry came to symbolize our national industrial demise. Billions of dollars and a huge chunk of the international market were lost to German and Japanese competitors, phoenixes risen from the ashes of war. American economic and industrial might dwindled in the face of global competition. American workers grew more and more disaffected, less caring about the quality of their work, and increasingly convinced that employers no longer cared about them and their families. Color TVs, VCRs, and other high-tech products invented in the postwar United States were made by willing and increasingly able manufacturers in Japan, Korea, and other countries, where business leaders readily learned the lessons of quality that the United States had seemingly forgotten.

In truth, Japanese industry had begun to apply statistical methodologies before the war, but had abandoned their efforts when the war began (Gabor 1990). Then, in 1946, a group of leading industrialists created a new organization, the Union of Japanese Scientists and Engineers (JUSE), to advance the cause of quality Japanese manufacturing. Japan's desperate straits were evident everywhere. There were precious few indigenous resources, a terrible housing shortage, and very little food. Japan could not afford to continue exporting junk. Only high-quality exports could bring Japan the hard currency required to import the food necessary to keep the Japanese people from starving in their devastated postwar environment.

In 1949, Deming was asked by the State Department to go to Japan to help that government prepare for the 1951 census because of the work Deming had done for the U.S. Census Bureau in the late 1940s. The Japanese government needed statistical population studies to know how desperate the housing shortages were, and how best to remedy the situation.

While in Japan, Deming met with his fellow statisticians. They had known for several years about Shewhart's work from handwritten, mimeographed translations of his writings. And many of them had attended a series of lectures on statistical process control sponsored by the Civil Communications Section (CCS) of the Allied command. The lectures were presented by three American quality control experts who had worked for Bell Labs and Western Electric. They stressed the importance of preventing mistakes before they happen rather than fixing them after the fact. High quality costs less, not more, they preached. They taught that high-quality supplies are required to make high-quality products.[2]

Total Quality in Japan

In 1950, JUSE, with the blessings of General Douglas MacArthur's office, invited Deming back to Japan to give a series of lectures on statistical quality control. MacArthur had his own good reasons for welcoming Deming's return. The Supreme Allied Commander wanted to communicate directly by radio with the Japanese people throughout the country. Japanese radios, however, were at the time highly unreliable. Deming, it was reasoned, could show the Japanese how to use statistical process control to make durable, reliable radios, which the Occupation Forces could place in at least 50 percent of all homes in Japan.

In his JUSE-sponsored lectures, Deming taught his Japanese audience how to use the Deming (PDSA) Cycle to constantly improve quality, and demonstrated the use of the statistical control charts pioneered by Shewhart, all of which he had done earlier for audiences in the United States. In *The Deming Management Method*, Mary Walton (1986) reports

---

[2]In his book *Managing Quality*, David A. Garvin (1988) of the Harvard Business School says that one of the CCS trainers, W.S. Magil, is sometimes "regarded as the father of statistical quality control in Japan. He first advocated its use in a lecture in 1945–46 and successfully applied its techniques to vacuum tube production at NEC in 1946."

that midway through his first lecture, Deming "was overcome with a sense of déjà vu. He was not talking to the right people. Enthusiasm for statistical techniques would burn out in Japan as it had at home unless he could somehow reach the people in charge."

Deming received support from Ichiro Ishikawa, president of JUSE and head of the *Keidanren*, the powerful Japanese Federation of Economic Organizations. Ishikawa wanted to impress upon Japanese industrial leaders the urgency of Japan's situation and the need for them to rethink their own management philosophies. Ishikawa invited 21 of the nation's top industrial executives to a dinner meeting with Deming. Many of them had been Ishikawa's students at the university, and still regarded him with the great reverence reserved for one's *sensei*, as is the deeply-rooted practice in Japan. Everyone showed up, and paid full attention to Deming, the tall, authoritative *gaijin*.[3]

At this first dinner with Japan's top industrial leaders, Deming drove home the point that, without the full support of top-level management, the quality revolution Japanese industry so desperately needed would be doomed from the start. It's not enough, Deming warned, to have a cadre of willing workers, all doing their best. The workers' efforts must be guided by the analysis of data and by what Deming would later call a system of profound knowledge, including a deep understanding of human psychology, learning theory, and variation within systems (Deming 1990). Deming told the Japanese to view their customers as the last and most important people on their production lines—a new idea for Japanese industrialists. He told them that quality is that which satisfies, even delights, the customer, and they must, therefore, go to their customers and ask them what they want. He suggested that they conduct door-to-door surveys and invest company resources in market research.

Deming emphasized the importance of eliminating production errors before they occur because defects require reworking, or scrapping, and are costly and wasteful. End-of-line inspection is also costly and wasteful because the inspector adds no value to the goods. In fact, Deming told his Japanese audiences that the inspector's presence often

---

[3]According to accepted Japanese tradition, a student's inferior position to his or her *sensei*, or teacher, does not change with the student's advancing age or accomplishments. It is expected that teachers will call students by their school names throughout life. Thus, the teacher's status permits him to call even the prime minister by an informal variation of his given name, while the prime minister must refer always to his teacher in the formal reverential term: *Sensei*. The word *gaijin* is Japanese for "foreigner."

suggests to the line workers that their mistakes will be caught down the line so they needn't pay close attention to the quality of their work. That, he argued, is a costly and self-defeating attitude.

At the end of his speech, Deming pledged to the assembled industrial leaders that, if they followed his advice and made quality their number one priority, consumers worldwide would be clamoring for Japanese products within five years. Even Deming himself privately thought his estimate optimistic. And yet, amazingly, it took only four years for his prophesy to begin to be realized.

In 1954, JUSE extended an invitation to lecture to a second noted American statistical expert, Joseph M. Juran. Juran's seminars reinforced Deming's earlier teaching. Juran told the Japanese that management, not the production worker, is most accountable for the organization's performance. In *Juran on Planning for Quality*, Juran (1988) stresses the need for management to carefully plan quality into the production process, to monitor the quality of products throughout the production process, and to improve quality at a rapid rate. Juran writes that good planning requires that a dependable process be developed. If the process is not dependable, goals will not be consistently achieved.

Juran (1988, p. 11) defines quality as "fitness for use" and "freedom from defects." He, like Deming, emphasizes the need to be attentive to the customers' perceptions of quality. The idea that the quest for quality must be an ongoing, never-ending process, is expressed graphically in Juran's "Spiral of Progress in Quality," which shows the following: Customers-Product Development-Operations-Marketing-Customers. The quality process begins and ends with the customer.

Juran told the Japanese to think of customers as "all persons who are impacted by our processes and our products," not just clients. He taught that there are internal as well as external customers. Juran (1988, p. 8) defines internal customers as "persons or organizations who are part of our company." External customers are "persons who are not part of our company but who are impacted by our products."

Juran (1988, p. 10) stresses the two-way relationship between customers and suppliers. "Customers provide their suppliers with requisitions, specifications, feedback on product performance, and so on. The customer becomes a supplier and the supplier becomes a customer."

About the time Juran was first visiting Japan, the Japanese were discovering the writings of another American quality expert, Armand Feigenbaum, who had served as the head of quality for General Electric. Feigenbaum was in contact with Hitachi, Toshiba, and other Japanese

JURAN'S SPIRAL OF PROGRESS IN QUALITY

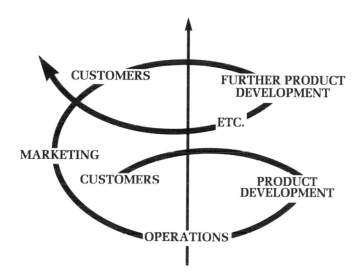

Reprinted with the permission of The Free Press, a Division of Macmillan, Inc., from JURAN ON PLANNING FOR QUALITY by J.M. Juran. Copyright © 1988 by Juran Institute, Inc.

companies. Those companies spread his ideas of "Total Quality Control," which "required the involvement of all functions in the quality process, and not simply manufacturing. Otherwise, quality would be inspected and controlled after the fact and not built in at an early stage" (Garvin 1988, p.183).

Deming, Juran, and Feigenbaum each spoke of the need for organizations to make quality their first priority. Their teachings were based on the idea that production goals cannot be consistently achieved unless attention is paid to the processes leading to those goals. Processes must be continually improved so that products can be continually improved.

The Japanese took to heart the lessons Deming, Juran, Feigenbaum, and their CCS colleagues from Bell Labs and Western Electric shared with them in the late 1940s and early 1950s. As a result, "quality" is now the byword of Japanese industry. To honor and celebrate the quality achievements of Japanese and foreign companies, JUSE established the Deming Prize, named in honor of their American *sensei*. The award is given annually to those companies demonstrating the greatest improvements in the quality of their processes and products.[4]

Total Quality Revisited in the United States

While the work of Deming, Juran, Feigenbaum, and other Americans was contributing to the economic miracle of postwar Japan, American industry and American society in general were happily—perhaps arrogantly—basking in the warm, reassuring glow of economic and military superpowerdom. Cars and other products were made not to last, but to self-destruct. "Planned obsolescence" became an accepted fact of life. Taylorism thrived. "How little quality can we get away with?" too often reflected the philosophy of American industry and commerce.

Disturbed by this attitude, Philip Crosby, an industrial consultant at ITT, joined his elder quality experts in preaching the gospel of "quality first" to American companies. He reinforced the idea that quality doesn't increase the cost of production, but lowers it. In *Quality Is Free*, Crosby (1980) argues that putting the best possible resources in at the front end of a process will more than pay for the investment later. Mistakes in business are costly, in terms of lost time, lost profits, lost customers, and lost opportunities for growth and learning. Compared with such costs, doing the right thing the first time around is considerably less expensive.

A rule of thumb in industry, known as The 1-10-100 Rule, illustrates this point. According to this rule of thumb, when and where a mistake is detected and corrected makes a big difference. If the error is discovered where and when the error is committed, it will cost 1 percent of what it might cost later if the defective product is discovered by the end-user who buys it in the marketplace. If the mistake is caught and corrected inside the factory, but after it leaves the department where the error was made, it might cost as much as 10 times what it could have cost if

---

[4]The American equivalent is the Malcolm Baldrige National Quality Award, established by an act of the United States Congress in 1987. JUSE asked Juran for permission to name an award after him, to be presented to the best of the Deming Prize recipients, but Juran declined, perhaps because he credits the Japanese themselves with the transformation they have achieved. Juran has said (Garvin 1988, p. 184): "I did indeed lecture in Japan as reported, and I did bring something new to them—a structured approach to quality. I also did the same thing for a great many other countries, yet none of these attained the results achieved by the Japanese. So who performed the miracle?"

corrected on the spot, but only 10 percent of what it might cost if discovered by the external customer. When mistakes are left undetected and uncorrected until they hit the marketplace, they can cost (in terms of money, trust and goodwill, and other resources) up to 100 times what they may have cost initially. The moral is this: Front-loading Quality in any process is always a better idea than trying to compensate for inadequacies later in the process. Invest in Quality now, or pay a lot more later on.

Finally, in the late 1970s American industry started taking note of Japanese successes in the international marketplace. The U.S. trade deficit was growing larger every year, as goods produced in this country were shunted aside even by domestic consumers in favor of goods made in more quality-conscious societies, including Japan, Korea, and Germany. Some U.S. executives went to Japan to nose around, trying to uncover the "secret" of Japanese success. There they saw groups of workers huddled in what seemed to be small discussion groups. These groups were the result of a nationwide "Quality Circle" movement that began to sweep Japan in the early 1960s. Quality Circles (QCs) are groups of workers who meet at their workplace to explore ways to improve their work and their work environment. QC members' efforts focus on their own self-development as well as development of others. A primary goal is to get all their fellow workers involved in the improvement process. The American executives who saw these QC's were determined to use them back in the United States.

Unfortunately, QC's didn't work in American business, where they were imposed upon workers from above. QC's in American factories and organizations soon turned into gripe sessions, and eventually were abandoned. The executives who brought the QC concept from Japan neglected to understand the larger Japanese culture of which QC's were only a small part. In Japan, all workers are honored. The company president has honor, the garbage collector has honor, the smallest merchant has honor. Japan is certainly a highly stratified and status-conscious society, but the willingness of workers to labor with great self-discipline for a common corporate cause is culturally ingrained in the Japanese work ethic. To not give one's best is dishonorable and disgraceful. To not give honor to others is also disgraceful. Japanese Quality Circles operate within such an ethos; American QC's generally did not. Also, Japanese workers were empowered to make changes in their work processes based upon discoveries made in their Quality

Circles; American workers were, in some cases, permitted only to offer suggestions to management, which largely ignored their ideas.

Kaoru Ishikawa, Ichiro Ishikawa's son and a noted quality expert in his own right, writes in *What Is Total Quality Control? The Japanese Way* that a number of differences exist between the Japanese and the Americans in their approaches to quality work. For example, in Japan, quality is every worker's business; in the United States, quality is often delegated to a division so that the idea of quality becomes compartmentalized within the organization. Some people are in charge of quality; most are not. Kaoru Ishikawa (1985, p. 25) says of Taylorism: "If people are treated like machines, work becomes uninteresting and unsatisfying. Under such conditions, it is not possible to expect products with good quality and high reliability. The rate of absenteeism and the rate of turnover are the measures one can use in determining the strengths and weaknesses of management style and worker morale in any company."

Ishikawa echoes the findings of recent surveys done in the United States when he suggests that the secret of success in business and in life is not found solely in the amount of money one earns, but also (and more importantly) in the satisfaction of doing one's work well, in the "happiness coming from cooperating with others and from being recognized by others," and in the joy of personal growth, which, he says, includes the following:

- experiencing the satisfaction that comes from being able to utilize one's own abilities to the fullest and from growing as a person;
- having self-confidence, and becoming a self-fulfilled person; and
- using one's own brain, working voluntarily, and in this way contributing to society (Ishikawa 1985, pp. 27–28).

Kaoru Ishikawa goes on to point out that the work group in Japan is like a family. Employees are hired for a lifetime, and this practice, according to Ishikawa (1985, p. 29), "can be a desirable system from the points of view of humanity, democracy, and management."[5] Such ideas have too infrequently found fertile soil in modern American culture, which is predicated upon tight top-down control, the arrogance of unlimited disparity in the compensation of employees and bosses, and a mindless preoccupation with bottom-line results even at the risk of organizational suicide.

---

[5]This practice is beginning to change in Japan as major corporations lay off workers during hard economic times.

The data were there for all to see. American productivity and the nation's economic health were clearly declining; marriages, corporate profits, and general civility were all heading south, and people just didn't seem to care about quality anymore. Something was going very wrong, and everyone wondered what it could be.

A part of the answer came in 1980, with the broadcast of an NBC TV documentary entitled "If Japan Can, Why Can't We?" The program focused on the work Deming had done in Japan, and the ways his teachings had helped the postwar Japanese economy to rebuild with dedication to quality and continuous improvement. The morning after the broadcast, Deming's phone began to ring off the hook as Ford, General Motors, and a host of other American companies sought his help, immediately if not sooner.

Deming's teachings, and those of other Quality consultants in business and education, continue to point our society, our businesses, and our educational systems in new and promising directions. Today, Schools of Quality—those schools that have dedicated themselves to continuous improvement for all of their people—are beginning to study and implement the philosophy of Total Quality, as expressed by Deming in his Fourteen Points (Deming 1986; see Appendix 3) and in what I have called the Four Pillars of Schools of Quality (See Chapter 4 and Appendix 2).

Deming encouraged educators to create school environments in which strong relationships of mutual respect and trust replace fear, suspicion, and division; and in which leadership from administrators and policymakers empowers students and teachers (as front-line workers of the school) to make continuous improvements in the work they do together. The development of everyone's "yearning for learning" is all-important in Schools of Quality; grades and other symbols of learning are far less significant. Deming, in fact, strongly opposed the use of grades altogether: "Abolish grades (A, B, C, D) in school, from toddlers up through the university. When graded, pupils put emphasis on the grade, not on learning" (Deming 1992).

The school, Deming emphasized, should be a place where students, teachers, administrators, and others are able to take pride and joy in their work. It is the responsibility of administrators—the top management of schools —to remove the barriers that prevent this from being the daily experience of students and teachers.

Mass inspection in the factory is inherently wasteful, Deming observed. Whenever inspection is relegated to the end of the production line, substandard products must be removed from the end of the assembly line, then sent back to the beginning for retooling or thrown on the trash heap. This practice, he observes, is possible (and wasteful) in the factory. But it is not possible to apply this solution to the young people who come through the educational process, failing at the end to achieve their potentials or, in some cases, even the minimum standards set by the school for graduation. Assessment should not wait until the end of the educational process, whether that process is a unit, a course, or the 13 years of schooling between kindergarten and the end of the senior year. Assessment for diagnostic and prescriptive purposes should inform every point along the line in the educational production process, providing teachers and students with a solid foundation for continuous improvement toward optimal success, rather than a judgmental "mark" or other end-of-the-line symbols of learning.

All of this cannot be done, Deming insisted, without the strongest possible leadership from the top of the organization. A "constancy of purpose for improvement," supported by vigorous programs of training and retraining, will enable school leaders to take decisive action to accomplish the transformation over time (See Appendix 3).

The message is clear. But is anyone really listening? What is blocking our path, and how can we identify and remove these obstacles? What keeps us from becoming better and better, continually fulfilling and expanding our potentials, growing in joy and wisdom every day?

The answers may not be readily apparent until we look carefully at the cultural paradigm into which we were born, raised, and now live. We are a part of our society's cultural paradigm, just as a fish is part of its watery environment. And yet, our cultural paradigm—our deeply ingrained societal and personal predispositions of thought, emotions, and behavior—are largely invisible to us. "Water? What water?" the fish might say if it could communicate with us. "I don't know anything about the water you speak of. All I know is that this is my home, and this is the way I live."

3

Learning a New Way to Swim

When my new friends Susan and Ted invited me and a few others to their home for an evening of slides taken on a trip to Europe, I was excited. I had travelled through some of the places on their itinerary so I was eager to discover their perspectives on the people they had met, the ways the people live, and the ideas they shared with Susan and Ted.

"Okay, now here's the first picture. Here we are at the airport, waving goodbye," Susan began.

"Our flight was two hours late," Ted added. We all commiserated. Airport delays: The scourge of modern travel.

"Okay, here we are in Europe. I think that's Big Ben behind us there. It's hard to tell. It was cloudy that day," Ted explained.

"Next picture!" Susan announced. "Oops! Ted, we should have taken this one out. Sorry, everybody. That's a blurry one." Ted scooped the slide from the tray.

"Okay, here I am in front of a church," Susan continued. "Where was this, honey?"

"Rome, I think," Ted replied. "The scenery was just spectacular!" We all agreed: Spectacular scenery.

This whirlwind tour went on for a while. Finally I asked, "What were the people like?"

"You mean the people on the tour?" Susan asked. "Oh, they were all very nice, very friendly folks."

"No," I replied. "I mean, what were the people like who live there? What kind of work do they do? What do they do in their spare time?"

Ted seemed mildly irritated by my questions, "We didn't have much time for that," he responded. "You know how tours can be—on the bus, off the bus, on the bus."

Susan shrugged and said, "Anyway, we *did* seven countries in ten days!"

It was as if Ted and Susan could now check off seven more countries on their list of experiences acquired. Great Britain? Check! France? Check! Luxembourg? Nope, next time! Metaphorically, I thought, they had just collected seven nations, and put them into their pockets for safekeeping. The slides served as proof of ownership.

I suspect that, for Susan and Ted, life's meaning has much to do with acquiring and possessing. The prominent psychologist Erich Fromm referred to this way of thinking and behaving as the "having mode" of living.

"The having mode of existence is not established by an alive, productive process between subject and object; it makes *things* of both object and subject. The relationship is one of deadness, not aliveness" (Fromm 1976). Thus, a rich opportunity for growth and learning and the expansion of one's universe may rationally be sacrificed for the things acquired, or for symbols of those things. It's impossible to actually carry the continent back home so symbolic slides must suffice. Fromm distinguishes this "having mode" from another way of living, which he calls the "being mode of existence."

Western culture is increasingly focused on *having*, not on *being* (and certainly not on *becoming*). This is the "water" in which we American fish swim, most often without knowing its depth and breadth, or the pressures it puts on us from all sides. The having mode is at the core of our daily lives, and it informs—or, more often, misinforms—our perceptions, thoughts, feelings, and behavior. This having mode lies at the heart of what remains of our production-oriented work ethic. It influences the ways we perceive and treat ourselves, how we love ourselves and others, the ways we learn and remember, and our ways of knowing and understanding. The having mode is well known to students and teachers.

Fromm points out that

> students in the having mode aim to hold onto what they "learned," either by entrusting it firmly to their memories or by carefully guarding their notes. They do not have to produce or

create anything new. In fact, having-type individuals feel rather disturbed by new thoughts or ideas about a subject, because the new puts into question the information they already have. Indeed, to one for whom having is the main form of relatedness to the world, ideas that cannot be pinned down (or penned down) are frightening—like everything else that grows and changes and, therefore, is not controllable" (Fromm 1976).

The having mode, expressed by scores of Western writers, thinkers, and artists, is grounded in the notion that living things are essentially unconnected unless their relationship is competitive, adversarial, and mutually exclusive. This perspective goes back as far as Aristotle, who divided all of human sensation into sight, taste, smell, touch, and hearing. Yet, today, we know that humans have more than thirty bodily sensory functions, virtually all of which are interconnected (Leonard 1978).

Aristotle and other great thinkers of ancient Greece perceived their world in logical dichotomies: good and bad, right and wrong, male and female, winners and losers. In this view of nature, polar opposites are perpetually at war with each other for ultimate control. Their mutual exclusivity makes life a contest in which only the stronger element of each dichotomy survive.

DICHOTOMIES

Us—Them
Right Answer—Wrong Answer
Life—Death
Male—Female
Winners—Losers
White—Black
Body—Mind
Intellect—Emotion
Pain—Pleasure

Students in the being mode, according to Fromm, develop a wider perspective than their having-mode peers:

Instead of being passive receptacles of words and ideas, they listen, they hear, and most important, they receive and they respond in an active, productive way. What they listen to stimulates their own thinking processes. New questions, new ideas, new perspectives arise in their minds. Their listening is an alive process. . . . They do not simply acquire knowledge that they can take home and memorize. Each student has been affected and has changed: each is different after [the lesson] than he or she was before it (Fromm 1976).

This view of the world springs from the ancient Confucian tradition, graphically represented by the yin-yang, an ancient oriental symbol of wholeness:

Like the polar opposite dichotomies, the yin-yang is divided into two parts. In the yin-yang, however, each half depends upon the other half for its existence. Neither has meaning without the other. Nothing can exist without its opposite. To know Good is impossible without knowing Evil. To know what is Wrong, one must also know what is Right. Each element is balanced by its opposite. Life consists not of adversarial dichotomies, but of *dualities*—polar opposites that add richness and meaning to one another.

Notice that within the light half of the yin-yang there is a dark dot, and within the dark half there is a light dot of the same size. This signifies that everything contains a small element of its opposite. In the evil that befalls each of us there are the seeds of good. From death springs life, from endings come beginnings. Thus, life is viewed as a cycle or spiral, a continuous wheel of existence known to the people of India as the Great Mandala. Life in the Eastern tradition is of one cloth, interconnected and neverending.

In this worldview, the integrity of the product—especially in the long term—is always dependent upon the integrity of the process used in getting to the product.

The following is a diagram of a single process. The beginning of the process is Point A. The goal, or product, is Point B. The line between the two points represents a series of moments during the process.

A- - - - - - - - - - - -> B

Point A (the beginning of the process) and Point B (the realization of the product, or goal, or result) are actually points in time. There are other points in time to the left of A, to the right of B, and between A and B. All of those points are also part of a larger, ongoing process, of which this A-B segment is only a small part.

- - - - - - -> A- - - - - - - - - - - - ->B - - - - - - ->

Product-oriented people focus only on the results at the end of the process (point B). They are comfortable in dichotomistic modes of thinking and acting, so they tend to view the end product as an objective separate from the entire process. If they concern themselves at all with the process leading to the objective, it is only to think of it as a nuisance, not as an opportunity for growth and learning. All effort is thus expended on the speedy acquisition of the goal. The product is viewed as a static end-point. Once the objective is "captured," it is held inviolable, protected against mutation and encroachment, and thus, kept from improvement. The value of the process is found solely in the results: The proof is in the pudding.

A- - - - - - - - - - - ->| B |

By viewing the product as a fixed end-point, product-oriented people figuratively capture the product and store it away in a box for safe keeping. The box I've drawn around Point B shows that the outcome is enclosed in this way, protected for all time. Ted and Susan put their "seven countries" into this sort of box. We educators have traditionally put students' test scores into a kind of box, too. The problem is, while students' grades stay permanently inscribed in the appointed boxes in teachers' gradebooks, the learning processes and products symbolized by those grades are constantly being transmuted: Some elements of the learning processes become incorporated into the students' ways of dealing with real life, while other "learnings" have a post-exam half-life of, perhaps, three minutes. Also, the grades in those gradebooks don't show how much the teachers—and their school as a "learning organization"—have learned through the process.

The person who is process-oriented understands the importance of setting worthy goals, but also knows that the process is what makes goals achievable. Process-oriented people, therefore, take great pains to plan the process carefully, and monitor and adapt the process constantly to ensure continuous improvement. They know that the quality of their input into the process will in large part determine the quality of the product, or output.

They view the product not as a static end-point, but as a dynamic access-point, leading to other processes and products.

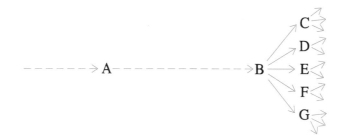

Process-oriented people assess the quality of the processes as well as the products that flow from those processes. This view reflects the fact that every process takes place within a network of other processes. This network is called a *system*. Elements of a system are interconnected, so each process affects other processes within the system. When all processes are of the highest possible quality, working synergistically (like the students in Bob's class or the players on his football team when "everything is clicking"), we can say that the system is *optimized*. Whenever any process within a system is functioning below its peak-performance level, or when elements of the system are working at cross-purposes or with only the product in mind, the entire system (including its processes) is *suboptimized*.

When a system is suboptimizing, it is most helpful to assess the entire system, including all of its processes. Shewhart identified two causes of system suboptimization: *random variation* and *assignable causes*, later designated by Deming as *common causes* of variation and *special causes* of variation. A common cause of variation is one that relates to the functioning of the system as a whole; a special cause of variation occurs when a process is failing within the system. Deming and others have suggested that, in any system, 85 percent or more of the reasons for suboptimization can be traced to the way the system is set up (failure due to common causes). Less than 15 percent of the failures are due to individual processes or people malfunctioning within a fully functioning system (failure due to special causes).

The implications for education are significant. The classroom teacher and his students are part of a learning system within the confines of the room, and they are part of a much larger system within the school building, which, in turn, is part of the school district, families and community, the state, the nation, and the world. The optimization of any one of these systems is dependent to some extent upon the functioning of the others because the processes of every system affect the entire system, positively or negatively. Every experience, inside and outside of the classroom, affects the learning that can take place in the classroom. According to Chester Finn, between birth and graduation from high school, a person spends only 9 percent of his or her life in school. Ninety-one percent of the young person's life is lived *outside* the school building. It is obvious that processes and systems outside the classroom affect the processes and systems within it.

What inputs are part of the process of growing up for today's young person? And what are the products of those processes? How are youngsters affected by television, advertisements, movies, the neighborhood, the kinds of food they eat, their family structures, and loving parental discipline or its absence? What about our culture's growing commercialization? The growing alienation of people from one another? The mounting pressures of time and money? What effects do these factors—all inputs from society into the systems of education—have on educators and students?

How do business successes and failures influence educators' ability to do their best possible work? Do educators and business people see each other as possible partners, or do they view one another in more dichotomistic terms? Do parents and teachers view one another as partners in the continuous improvement of children's lives? Do parents accept their rightful role as the primary teachers of their children, and are teachers supportive of that role for parents?

How do state and federal regulations affect the work that administrators do, and how does all of this provide inputs into the micro-learning system of the classroom teacher and her students?

Educators must consider the ramifications of these and other issues. When we neglect to factor these inputs into our equations in school restructuring, strategic planning, curriculum design, teacher training, and the other work of our profession, we very surely design suboptimization and failure into our systems.

Total Quality Management provides educators with a conceptual framework for addressing these issues in our schools. TQM gives us a philosophy and a set of tools to understand—through data analysis—what our systems are made of, what they are capable of doing, and the reasons and ways suboptimization is taking place. Unfortunately, most organizations—including businesses and schools all around the world—still function in a Tayloresque manner with hierarchical, top-down authoritarian power structures based upon compliance, control, and command; little true empowerment of front-line workers to create, monitor, and control their own work processes; little real participation by workers in the governance of the organization; and more attention to end products than to the processes essential to increased productivity.

In this virtual prescription for suboptimization, the efforts of an organization are not focused on educating the customer about quality or delighting the customer, or even serving the customer. Suppliers are left to their own devices and are often viewed as threats or as inconsequential to the work of the organization. People within the organization do not treat one another as essential suppliers and customers, so the synergy that might "make things click" never even begins.

An organization with such a dichotomistic, product-focused orientation makes it difficult for people associated with the organization to learn from each other. What should be a growing, continuously improving, optimizing, learning organization is instead a place where people communicate less and less with each other while they grow more and more disaffected from one another, from their bosses, and from their work. This situation is particularly ironic and tragic when the erstwhile "learning organization" is a school, where the optimization of the system is so crucial for our collective future, as well as for the personal futures of our children.

Peter Senge (1990, p. 5) points out in *The Fifth Discipline: The Art and Practice of the Learning Organization* that "as the world becomes more complex and dynamic, work must become more 'learningful.' It's no longer sufficient to have one person learning for the organization, 'figuring it out' from the top, with everyone else following the orders of the 'grand strategist.' To truly excel in the future, organizations will have to tap the commitment and capacity to learn of people at *all* levels in an organization." A learning organization, says Senge (1990, p. 4), is "continually expanding its capacity to create" its future. In the language of Total Quality, a true learning organization optimizes its entire system—including processes and products—by empowering everyone, especially front-line workers—students and teachers in the case of schools—to continuously improve their work.

Teachers and students, as the schools' front-line workers, must be empowered to put forth their best efforts and understand the processes, systems, and opportunities for continual growth and improvement. In fact, an essential aspect of learning how to improve thinking and learning capabilities is learning how to expand our perceptual awareness. Empathy and the development of a wider perceptual field are linked. People who are aware of their own thoughts, feelings, and behaviors are often best able to understand the thoughts, feelings, and behaviors of others. Greater awareness of the whole, of the system of processes (of which the individual is a part), is a natural extension of the quest for continuous improvement, which is at the heart of Total Quality. In a chapter entitled "Toward Process-Oriented Persons," the University of Maryland's Louise Berman (1968) writes: "Highly process-oriented persons do not stagnate under the debris of nonessential or nonmeaningful aspects of life. They see purposes to the degree of change and movement they plan for themselves." They are in the process of self-actualization, otherwise known as continuous improvement.

It baffles me that the process of learning in today's classrooms so infrequently includes time for reflection by teachers and students on the optimization of the learning they do together. The routine is always the same: Begin the unit, teach the unit, give the students a test, correct the test, return the test, review the "right" answers with the class, collect the tests, and record the grades. Then move on the next unit. If we continue this practice, how will students learn to use experiences from past units to improve the work they do on future units?

To help students engage in constant improvement, we must make the teacher-student learning system the focal point of instruction so that the ways teachers and students interact in the learning process can be continually fine-tuned.

Educators who focus on this teacher-student interaction and understand and apply this process/systems philosophy know that it requires a lifestyle change. It takes a dedication to the process of continuous improvement, for oneself and for others in the "system"—whether that system is a group of friends, a workplace, a family, or any other set of interconnections in life. When you apply this philosophy of Total Quality to yourself and your relations with other people, places, and things, you take on a kind of interpersonal, planetary stewardship. For many of us "American fish," this philosophy provides a new and challenging way to swim in the waters of our families, our workplaces, and our communities.

4

Reconsidering the Better Mousetrap

"**B**uild a better mousetrap, and the world will beat a path to your door!" Remember that old adage?

Mousetraps are good to have around. *If* you have mice.

The key idea, however, is not to invent a better way to kill mice, but to discover a way to not have mice around in the first place. In TQM parlance this means it's better to create high-quality processes so your system operates optimally, rather than putting up with unwanted products you will need to "inspect out" at the end of the production line. If you can fix the system so those pesky mice don't find their way to your domicile, you won't need a better mousetrap. In fact, you won't need any kind of mousetrap.

Total Quality Management is not a program for building a better mousetrap in a business, school, or community organization. In fact, Total Quality is not really a program at all. It isn't a panacea for curing all the ills of your organization's staff, or those of the community or anyone or anything else. And it most certainly isn't a "flavor of the month" reform effort. It is not something you will "do" this month or this year, as Susan and Ted "did" their seven countries in ten days and then put their experiences and their symbolic slides aside.

Total Quality is, as we have seen, a new way of thinking and living that pervades all aspects of life. When the Quality Philosophy is fully implemented in an organization, it becomes the heart and soul of the organization's way of operating. It becomes the new "water" in which the organization's fish swim. It is accepted as "the way things are done around here" by everyone in the organization, and by everyone who influences and is influenced by the organization's system. Total Quality requires consistent effort by the entire team, working together toward common objectives based upon an accepted vision and mission, and using quantitative and qualitative data to measure how well the system is meeting the needs of all stakeholders inside and outside of the organization. How long must this commitment to Total Quality go on? As W. Edwards Deming has said: "Forever!" (Gottlieb 1984). What we're really talking about, of course, is nothing less than a paradigm shift. In *Future Edge*, Joel Barker (1992, p. 31) quotes Adam Smith's definition of a paradigm as "a shared set of assumptions. The paradigm is the way we perceive the world: water to the fish. The paradigm explains the world to us and helps us to predict its behavior."

In *The Aquarian Conspiracy*, Marilyn Ferguson (1980, p. 228) describes a new paradigm of education, which "looks to the nature of learning rather than methods of instruction. Learning, after all . . . is the process by which we have moved every step of the way since we first breathed; the transformation that occurs in the brain whenever new information is integrated, whenever a new skill is mastered. Learning is kindled in the mind of the individual. Anything else is mere schooling."

Schooling has tended to mirror business in its adherence to Taylor-esque qualities. Arthur C. Clarke (1986, p. 76) points out in *July 20, 2019: Life in the 21st Century* that there will need to be a paradigm shift in education's basic emphasis: "Our current educational system evolved to produce workers for the Industrial Revolution's factory-based economy, for work that requires patience, docility, and the ability to endure boredom. Students learned to sit in orderly rows, to absorb facts by rote, and to move as a group through the material regardless of individual differences in learning speed."

"But," Clarke points out, "no factory jobs will be left in 2019. Except for a few technicians to watch over control panels, tomorrow's factories will be automatic, with computers directing robot workers."

Former Barnard College President Ellen Futter (Clarke 1986, p. 76) suggests: "We must give [students] certain key intellectual skills—analytical thinking, critical thinking, the ability to make judgements, to reason quantitatively, to balance opposed points of view. We must focus more on how to learn, how to think."

In such a learning environment, the school relinquishes its past role as a delivery system for discreet and often fragmented bits of data in the guise of curriculums. The school becomes, instead, a place where people (of all ages) cultivate their innate "yearning for learning," as Deming would say. Nothing is more important than keeping that yearning alive. Nothing is more important than cultivating a love of learning, of personal growth, and of getting better and better while helping others to do the same.

In the new paradigm of learning, schools learn how to create processes that encourage the continuous improvement of one's abilities, the expansion of one's interests, and the growth of one's character. Such an education is good for the individual student, good for the economy, and good for the commonweal we call society (Bonstingl 1992, p. 67). However, according to management consultant Robert F. Lynch (1991, p. 64), today "our entire educational system is designed to teach people to do things the one right way as defined by the authority figure. We are taught to recite what we hear or read without critically interacting with the information as it moves in and out of short-term memory. In this exchange, the information leaves no tracks, and independent thinking skills are not developed."

In *A Whack on the Side of the Head: How To Unlock Your Mind for Innovation*, Roger von Oech (1983, p. 21) asks, "Where do you learn how to think? One important source is your formal schooling. . . . Your educational training gives you many of the concepts you use to order and understand the world." Thus, the paradigm of the school becomes for many the paradigm of life.

Von Oech continues:

> Much of our educational system, however, is geared toward teaching people the one right answer. By the time the average person finishes college, he or she will have taken over 2,600 tests, quizzes, and exams. . . . Thus, the right answer approach becomes deeply ingrained in our thinking. This may be fine for some mathematical problems where there is in fact only one right answer. The difficulty is that most of life doesn't present itself in this way. Life is ambiguous; there are many right answers—all depending on what you are looking for. But if you think there is only one right answer, then you will stop looking as soon as you find one.

Looking to the authority figure for the one right answer can be deadly in the business world, where a variety of competing "right answers" vie for implementation and adoption by producers and consumers alike. In my article "The Total Quality Classroom" (Bonstingl 1992), I tell the story of a new employee, a college student whom my friend Jim had hired to work at his family-owned Italian restaurant. One day, this new employee, Lisa, stunned Jim with this question: "How many mushrooms should I put on a 12-inch pizza?"

Jim thought it was a strange question, but Lisa explained that at her previous job as a pizzamaker for one of the big chain restaurants, she and her fellow employees had to follow a thick rulebook. And the rulebook specified the exact number of mushroom slices for every size pizza.

"She wanted the right answer," Jim told me. "She wanted *my* right answer, not the customer's right answer."

It's an easy step from seeking teachers' and professors' right answers to seeking employers' right answers. How many of our students come through their schooling believing that the end-user of their work is the teacher? How many young people realize that their education is *their* education, a tool for what should be their own self-improvement? "How many mushrooms on a 12-inch pizza?" Frederick Winslow Taylor would have been delighted!

Jim thought for a moment, then replied with his own question (Socrates would have been pleased): "Do *you* like pizza?"

"Sure, I like pizza," Lisa responded.

"Okay," Jim answered, "how many mushrooms do *you* like on *your* pizzas? Just do for your customers what you would like if you were them. You decide!"

Jim's central tenet, one shared with every employee in the restaurant's thorough and ongoing training process, is simple: Always keep the customer first in mind. Customers have, as Lisa would soon find out, a wide variety of preferences. There were lots of "right answers" for her to find out from them. Lots of different, and often *differing*, perspectives to consider.

In the world of the future, with increasing diversity and global interconnections, our young people will need to be as comfortable with answers from people who live halfway around the world as they are with the opinions of their friends and neighbors. The "one right answer" just isn't right anymore. Dichotomistic, product-oriented modes of thought and behavior do not fit the needs of the global village, which must be viewed as one unified system of diverse people and processes.

Today, in Schools of Quality, a new process-oriented paradigm of continuous learning and improvement is beginning to replace the old Tayloresque, product-oriented, fear-driven paradigm of teaching and testing (See Appendix 4).

William Glasser, the psychiatrist who has spent his lifetime developing more humane, more effective ways of teaching and learning, observes that Quality-oriented schools are possible only within environments of trust and cooperation. It is imperative that the school climate meet, on a constant basis, its people's basic human needs for physical and psychological survival, love and inclusion, power and impactfulness, freedom within structure, and the fun of exploration and learning. Glasser's teachings form the essential psychological foundation for human development in Schools of Quality (see Glasser 1992).

School leaders with whom I have worked to create Schools of Quality agree that there are four essential elements of this new Total Quality educational paradigm. I call these four characteristics the Four Pillars of Quality:

1. A customer-supplier focus
2. Constant dedication to continuous improvement
3. A process/systems approach
4. Strong and consistent Total Quality leadership

Each of these Four Pillars has many implications for the work of schools and school leaders.

A Customer-Supplier Focus

As with other fiscally based enterprises, schools are in business to satisfy their customers and to maximize opportunities to serve and delight them. Every thriving business must satisfy the needs of not only *external* customers (those who buy and use the organization's product or service), but also *internal* customers (people within the organization who help to create the service or product and those who are affected by their work). Within an organization, all workers must collaborate with their suppliers—the people who provide the materials used in the production process—to make sure the suppliers' work meets the internal customer's specific needs. Everyone inside every organization is a supplier as well as a customer, and therefore chains and networks of partnership and mutual support (externally as well as internally) must be built to optimize the effectiveness of the organizational system.

In Schools of Quality, and also in their communities, everyone is both a customer and a supplier. A clear, personalized understanding of these roles is essential for optimal systemic improvement to take place.

Our schools' customers are, primarily, our students and their families. They are, or should be, the main beneficiaries of our schools' work. As trustees of young students, parents are initially *primary* customers of their children's school, but as children grow and mature, parents necessarily make the transition to *secondary* customers of the school, enabling their children as *primary* customers of the school to take control of their own educational journeys.

Parents and families, as suppliers to the schools, entrust their tax monies and their children to the schools' care. Parents are also, in a certain sense, suppliers who must provide their children with their very first lessons in responsibility, understanding, and compassion, as well as the pre- and post-natal psychological and physiological nutrition required for mental and physical health. It is the responsibility of Schools of Quality and their communities to work with these parent-family suppliers to optimize children's potentials to benefit from the learning processes provided at school.

Students, working alongside their teachers, are not only the primary customers of the schools, but also the schools' frontline workers. Students, as workers, produce their own continuous improvement of abilities, interests, and character. Their main focus must be the constant, authentic, and long-term improvement of self and others, rather than the acquisition of grades and other symbols of short-lived learning.

Teacher-student teams are the customers of the school administrators, who are the suppliers of a learning environment and educational context in which human potential is maximized and barriers to students' and teachers' pride and joy in working together are eliminated from the processes of the system.

Teachers are suppliers and customers of one another. The 5th grade teacher team finds out what the 6th grade teacher team expects of students. Effective, ongoing communication between building sites makes it possible for teachers at the elementary, middle, and high school levels to modify their work with students to better prepare them for the academic and social challenges they will encounter in future years.

The school board, setting the larger context for optimization of the school district as a working system, supplies policies that empower and enable their internal customers, the site and district administrators, to create a true learning organization in which micro-management is put aside in favor of genuine site-based management. As customers of the school board, administrators at every level must feel free to discuss their needs honestly and openly with the board, without reservation, intimidation, or fear. School board members and school administrators trained in Quality principles and practices view themselves as teammates of one another and of teachers, students, staff, parents, families, businesses, and community members—all of whom are, or should be, partners in the progress of the schools' people and processes.

At the local, state, and federal levels, agencies whose policies influence school board and administration practices are suppliers of policy contexts to school boards and administrators. District school officials must help higher policymaking agencies view themselves as suppliers and teammates of school district and site administrators. Here again, the old Tayloresque model of compliance, control, and command gives way to a new model of teamwork and mutual dedication to continuous improvement of the entire system and its people and processes.

Secretarial staffs, bus drivers, groundskeepers, and other employees of the school district are also part of the overall system, and play active roles as suppliers and customers of each other and of teachers, students, administrators, and other stakeholders in Schools of Quality.

The most successful Quality-focused organizations are careful to create effective feedback loops to build ongoing partnerships with their customers and suppliers. Feedback loops enable us to know what our customers expect of us, and they help us to provide our suppliers with information about what we need in order to best serve our customers. Here is an example of a simple feedback loop:

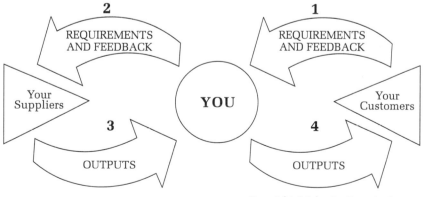

Copyright © John Jay Bonstingl 1996

As you study this feedback loop, ask yourself: Who are my internal and external customers, the people who use my work? What do they need and expect from me? How do I know what their needs and expectations are, and how can I get feedback from them on a continuing basis, so I'm better able to serve them?

Then ask yourself: Who are my internal and external suppliers, the people whose work I use in the process of serving my customers? How can I best communicate my needs to my suppliers on a continuing basis, so that we can work together to meet my customers' needs?

School leaders who spend time and other resources developing highly personalized customer-supplier relationships inside and outside of the school building reap abundant rewards in terms of the continuous improvement of the system and its processes. For example, administrators at Wilde Lake High School in Columbia, Maryland, are working closely with local businesspeople who employ Wilde Lake students after school hours. The employers join forces with the school to help their student employees improve their schoolwork. At the same time, the school gets valuable information from those businesses, in their role as current and prospective employers of Wilde Lake students, concerning the strengths and shortcomings of those young people's academic preparation for the world of work.

Other Schools of Quality determine what their customers and suppliers need by conducting focus groups with parents, students, administrators, teachers and other staff members, business people, and taxpayers who meet and critique the processes and products of the school system. Still others conduct surveys of staff, parents, community members, and students to find out how well the school and district are meeting the needs of all stakeholders. As Carl Marburger, who pioneered the creation of effective school-parent-community networking processes as co-founder of the National Committee for Citizens in Education, has said, schools and their stakeholders must move "beyond the bake sale" solutions to create positive, ongoing relationships of understanding and support *before* crises occur (Henderson et al. 1987). Focus groups, surveys, and other data-gathering and power-sharing instruments serve not only to inform school leaders and their staffs about the perceptions stakeholders have of the schools, but also to invite people to make personal contributions of time, ideas, energies, and even "yes" votes on essential bond issues—all of which help to make possible the school's continuous improvement process. That brings us to the second of the Four Pillars of Quality.

Constant Dedication to Continuous Improvement

In Total Quality organizations, including Schools of Quality, all individuals must be dedicated to self-improvement and the betterment—little by little, day by day—of other people in their spheres of influence. This, as we have seen, is what the Japanese call *kaizen*, a never-ending journey of improvement for oneself, one's family and friends, workmates, community, and, ultimately, the world. An idealistic and optimistic philosophy, to be sure, but one that actually works.

Rather than encouraging students to explore hidden talents and to build on previous successes and understandings, our tradition of schooling has all too often focused on students' failures, inadequacies, and limitations. The bell curve and other devices that create artificial scarcities of student success result in artificial limitations of individual and schoolwide success. Success in such a system is, by design, limited to a few "winners," while others are made to consider themselves and their work as mediocre or inferior.

While many traditional schools still view learning as a collection of linear, consecutive segments of one-way communication, Schools of Quality view the learning process as a spiral, with students' and teachers' energies directed toward unlimited continuous improvement, similar to Juran's Spiral of Progress in Quality, or a spiral-shaped PDSA Cycle, or a continuous Experience Pattern (perception—conceptualization—thought—action—reaction—perception, etc.) as shown in the diagram below (adapted from Bonstingl 1996).

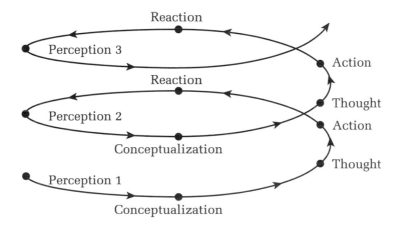

In this view of continuous learning, rather than serving as silent tabulae rasae or empty vessels to be filled by teachers, texts, and tests, students use their prior knowledge and understanding as the foundation for construction of new learning and the constant refinement of developing intelligences. The philosophy of constructivism supports this view. According to constructivism, *learning is the construction of meaning.* The meaning of the present moment is understood based on the meanings of past moments. Everyone who reads this book, therefore, will understand its meaning in a way that is somewhat different from the way every other reader understands it. Everyone's worldview is different because everyone's Experience Patterns throughout life are different, as are the meanings we attach to those experiences.

The spiral of learning is an old and familiar construct in the field of education. Hilda Taba (1971) introduced concept spirals in instructional practice a generation ago. Indeed, Socrates' approach might be viewed as essentially spiral, with the focus on questions leading students to ever-higher levels of understanding. Schools of Quality worldwide conceptualize optimal learning processes as spirals of continuous improvement. In the Alternative Secondary School for Economics, Hungary's first privately funded, teacher-operated secondary school, the motto is "We are for the tadpoles." Growth is seen as a spiral, in which the school's "tadpoles" eventually develop into "frogs." The process of being a tadpole comes first, and has great internal integrity.

At the Centro de Educacion Natural e Integral (CENI) of Montevideo, Uruguay, students and teachers join together in a spiral journey of learning that takes them from the very concrete to the very abstract. "The children live and breathe the spirit of cooperation and sharing. . . . Good work is that which results in learning new information, is healthy for the body, and is shared by or offered to the group," according to Jeanette Stanko, who has done extensive on-site research into the operation of the school.

> In a learning environment where the children's prior knowledge is respected and valued and where they are allowed to manipulate, control, and question what they are learning about . . . .
> In this community, the teacher is more like a group guide or enabler, providing and setting up the learning experiences, but allowing the students to experiment, question, observe, and manipulate the environment at their own pace, in their own way (Stanko 1991).

In Schools of Quality, learning for everyone—students, teachers, administrators, and other staff—is viewed as a journey, not a series of destinations. Life itself is viewed as a journey with intrinsic merit if it is undertaken with a zest for living, a love of oneself and others, and a yearning for learning. Thus, the School of Quality is a true learning community in which everyone is dedicated to continuous improvement of self, others, and the processes and systems of everyday life. In the classroom, teachers and students take time at the end of each unit to figure out how they did their work together, and how their collective and individual efforts might be fine-tuned in the following unit to maximize success and optimize collective and individual learning processes and systems.

Just as employees of many "learning" companies in Japan and the United States come together in Quality Circles on a regular basis to study ways of improving their individual and collective efforts, at some Schools of Quality, teachers, administrators, and other staff members are beginning to meet in QC's to discover ways of improving individually and collectively in their work with each other and with the students and other stakeholders.

Teacher QC's most often meet on school time to discuss new ideas garnered from readings about their discipline and education in general. Often, QC's or their equivalent take the form of cross-disciplinary teacher discussions about methods, materials, and student progress. Such discussions often include *benchmarking*—monitoring successful educational experiments from all around the world as possible models from which to learn and adopt new ideas for local educational environments and processes. Benchmarking is gaining favor in education, as well as in the world of business, because it encourages continuous improvement by everyone, allowing standards of performance to rise rapidly.

In Napa, California, cross-disciplinary groups of teachers at a Quality middle school have a common planning period each day while their students are taking physical education classes. Every tenth day, students are dismissed early, giving teacher teams the entire afternoon to plan and discuss ways of improving their individual and collective efforts toward continuous learning and improvement for themselves and their students. This common study and discussion time is what makes the school work—"the genius of the plan," says the school's principal—and it is well worth the time invested.

This *kaizen* focus also extends to faculty meetings at the school. There are two after-school faculty meeting seach month, hosted on a revolving basis by a faculty member in a designated classroom area. During these meetings, the host teachers share new ideas about instructional methods, classroom environments, curriculums and materials, and discuss issues of common concern. Faculty members walk away from these meetings energized and rededicated to the success of their common cause, the optimization of teacher and student successes.

Quality Circles work for students, too. At a Quality middle school in Maryland, small groups of students work in Support Teams known as "S-Teams" (a play on the word esteem). S-Team members pledge to support each others' efforts toward continuous academic and personal improvements. They become, in many cases, like families. The school's S-Teams present their improvement plans at schoolwide student government assemblies, and then work together to make their plans into reality (Bonstingl 1991, pp. 572, 575).

At Carder School in Corning, New York, another kind of continuous improvement process is taking place. It is called the Koalaty Kid Project. Originated by the spirited Carder staff more than a decade ago, Koalaty Kid is now an important part of schools throughout North America. The belief that "every kid is a Koalaty Kid" is reinforced in many ways. In Nazareth, Pennsylvania, students and teachers use Quality tools such as affinity charts and fishbone diagrams (see Appendix 1) to figure out ways of making the lunchroom experience more efficient and pleasant for everyone. In Noble, Oklahoma, students delight in one another's successes at monthly recognition assemblies. In Brampton, Ontario, parent volunteers make weekly visits to the school to read aloud with children. In Koalaty Kid schools, "I caught you being good!" is a favorite slogan.

The Koalaty Kid program, coordinated by the American Society for Quality, has resulted in higher attendance, improved test scores, markedly increased student interest in reading, and an environment of empowerment and enthusiasm for administrators, teachers, students, and the business and community people who are encouraged to drop by and read with students.

Since its inception in the 1980s, Koalaty Kid has grown by leaps and bounds, and now draws interest from educators and parents around the world. David B. Luther, former chairman of the American Society for Quality, wrote in the first **Koalaty Kid Manual** (1991) that implementing this successful program "involves a team approach that includes not only teachers and administrators, but also students, parents, volunteers, and business partners."

Continuous improvement is an everyday part of life in Schools of Quality. At Beachwood Middle School, located in a suburb of Cleveland, Ohio, there is no failure. According to principal Edward Bernetich, "failure is simply not an option for our students." A few years ago, district superintendent Paul Williams and the school board became increasingly concerned that Beachwood students who were capable of high-quality work were "choosing not to succeed." Many were willing to receive low or failing marks, and seemed unconcerned about retention and other negative consequences. Parents, staff, and students met to resolve this dilemma.

Today, Beachwood Middle School operates under what they call their "A-B-C-Incomplete" policy to ensure that every student will succeed. Students who earn a grade lower than C receive a grade of "Incomplete" and must attend mandatory Saturday School until the "Incomplete" is raised to at least a C grade. By the end of the third year of operation, less than 5 percent had an "Incomplete." The A-B-C-I initiative, according to Principal Bernetich, "reinforces our deeply held belief that every child must learn how to succeed in school and in life." Little wonder that Beachwood Middle School is a two-time recipient of the U.S. Department of Education's Blue Ribbon Schools Award. This brings us to the third of my Four Pillars of Quality.

A Process/Systems Approach

Quality results in schools, as in business, come from quality processes and systems. In Schools of Quality, everyone understands that improvement of student outcomes can only be achieved, over the long run, when learning processes are being continuously improved by those on the front lines—teacher-student teams—and when the entire system supporting those processes is being continuously improved by administrators who create the context for optimal success within the school. Learning, by its very nature, transcends the school. Schools of Quality prepare young people for life-*long*, life-*wide*, and life-*deep* learning — three-dimensional learning that pervades every aspect of life's journey.[1]

---

[1] I am indebted to Professor Jost Reischmann of the University of Tübingen, Germany, for sharing his concept of *life-wide life-deep* learning with me.

All of the school's internal and external customers and suppliers, including all of its stakeholders, must be viewed as part of the school's operational system because each person's actions affect everyone else in the system. Total Quality Management tools and techniques, such as flowcharts and cause-effect diagrams, can be helpful in discovering who all of the "players" in the system really are, and what influences they have on the system. As members of the system begin to realize their essential interconnectedness, they can better understand what roles they play in fulfilling the potentials of the school and its people (see Appendix 1).

The most successful Schools of Quality build strong linkages with major stakeholders, recognizing them as essential contributors to the schools' ongoing improvement processes. In Madison, Wisconsin, several neighboring school systems have joined forces with civic and business organizations and hospitals to form the Madison Area Quality Improvement Network (MAQIN), which works actively in various ways to support the schools' continuous improvement processes. In El Paso, Texas, there is a wonderful Head Start program that should be the model for early childhood programs throughout the world. Nearly a decade ago, Blanca Enriquez, the energetic and visionary director of the program, embraced the Quality Philosophy for herself personally and for her entire organization, in order to give her clients—thousands of mostly poor Hispanic children and their families—a high-quality head start on life. Mrs. Enriquez has used her considerable leadership skills to bring the entire community on board as active partners and supporters. As a result, her successes are prized by the community's families, business and civic leaders, and local reporters who help spread the word about this model of quality dedication in action.

The same process/systems orientation necessary for Schools of Quality to establish networks of support in their quest for *kaizen* at a macro level is essential for learning and improvement to be optimized at the micro level, within each student. Research at the University of California (Brown 1975) has consistently shown that the deepest, most long-lasting learning takes place when it is *confluent* learning, merging the affective, cognitive, and psychomotor dimensions of learning. One of my first students described it this way: Pointing to his head and then his heart, he told me, "Mr. B., if you want to get me here, you gotta get me *here* first!" We now know that the three elements of the personal internal learning system are interlinked, and they work as processes within the larger human system. Yet, so much of our work with students, particularly at the upper grade levels and in postsecondary institutions, is focused on the cognitive realm. In Schools of Quality, caring environments are created by everyone, so that the heart can more easily join the head in the processes of *kaizen.*

Now let's look at our fourth and final Pillar of Quality.

Strong and Consistent Total Quality Leadership

For school leaders, this is the most important of the four essential characteristics of Schools of Quality. In the first of his Fourteen Points (see Appendix 3), Deming established the preeminent need for management to "create constancy of purpose for the improvement of product and service." Quality, insisted Deming, cannot and must not be delegated. Responsibility for quality processes, systems, and outcomes rests with management. Workers, acting by themselves, cannot create the systemwide conditions under which quality processes take place. That is the job of management, which is entrusted with the responsibility of fully adopting this new Total Quality philosophy throughout the organization, building relationships of trust from the top down, empowering and enabling frontline workers to continuously improve by removing the barriers to their natural joy and pride of workmanship, and garnering the necessary resources to provide ongoing training in Total Quality principles and practices.

Most importantly, management must drive fear out of the organization. The old fear-based Taylor system of compliance, control, and command has no place in the modern workplace—business or school—where people must think creatively, work in self-directed teams, and build partnership cultures of mutual support for everyone's continuous improvement. Leading is helping, coaching, and supporting, not threatening, ranking, or punishing (See Appendix 4).

Because of these redefined leadership responsibilities, administrators and other school leaders are essential players in initiating and maintaining the transformation process required to build Schools of Quality. And, because the journey is neverending, school leaders must be enabled and supported by all of the school's stakeholders in their continuing efforts to make the school better and better, day by day, year by year.

5

Defining the Real Business of Schools of Quality

If you are considering a Quality transformation process in your school or district, you're probably wondering where you should start. There are many good pathways to building Schools of Quality. It is important that you craft one specifically for your own special circumstances, taking into account the primary needs and wants of your stakeholders in the school and community. Your work will necessarily be based on your community's unique culture, history, and demographic and socio-economic make-up and trends. These are the first and most important considerations when beginning any Quality journey.

As a result of all the research and writing I have done on the worldwide Quality movement over the past several years, I am convinced that educators should not consider investing the considerable time, energy, and resources required to build a Quality transformation in our schools and communities until they first lay the necessary ground-work with all their stakeholders.

Developing ongoing partnerships with our suppliers and customers (both internal and external to the school and school system), building fear-free environments in which failing doesn't mean you are a failure, constantly improving ourselves while helping others in our spheres of influence to do the same—all these wonderful aspects of a true Quality transformation are irrelevant and not worthy of our serious consideration unless we *first* ask ourselves three basic questions, questions that enlightened businesspeople have recently begun to ask themselves, often with surprising results. Unless we answer these three questions with very specific kinds of responses, our Quality journey is improbable, perhaps even counterproductive to our current philosophies of education and modes of operation.

Question #1: What business are we *really* in? When the folks at Xerox—from the CEO to the custodians—began to meet in small cross-departmental teams focusing on the long-term systemic improvement of their company and their own work within the company, this at first appeared to be a dumb question. *What business are we really in?* Why, we're in the copier business, of course. It's obvious, isn't it? Doesn't the whole world call the process of document production by our own name: "Xeroxing"?

As they began to dig deeper into the meaning of their work, however, they concluded that the real business of Xerox was not making pieces of machinery called copiers. Xerox customers, they concluded, don't want just another machine taking up space in the office. What people really want is a quick and easy way to produce high-quality documents—and speedy, efficient, friendly service whenever it is needed.

Today, Xerox defines itself as "the document company"—a paradigm shift that has enabled Xerox to succeed in winning many new customers, delighting their old customers, and earning the Malcolm Baldrige National Quality Award in 1989. The folks at Xerox now believe their real business is helping customers learn how to be more and more successful in the production and management of their documents, so those customers are better able to run their businesses effectively and bring delight to *their* customers. Xerox wins when its customers (and customers' customers) win.

To gain valuable insights into their own work, the people of Xerox spend considerable time and resources on the process of *benchmarking*, investigating how other businesses known for their excellent processes, services, and products continually improve what they do to satisfy and delight all the people they serve, from coworkers internally to end-users externally. Some of the most valuable insights come from businesses outside of Xerox's own field of document production. "Great ideas are great ideas, no matter where they come from," as one Xerox representative told me.

Could we benefit from asking ourselves this same essential question, applying it to our work in education? What business are we educators really in? The answer may at first seem as self-evident as the initial answer the Xerox people gave. We may well say: "Why, we're in the business of teaching, of course." But whenever our young people don't learn, for whatever reasons, can we truly say that we have taught them?" We may say: "Why, we're in the business of educating young people to be successful, of course." Yet many educators still hold onto philosophies and practices that effectively divide students into winners and losers, even in the elementary grades and certainly at the secondary and university levels, by constructing artificial scarcities of success such as the bell curve.

The new paradigm of education encourages us to see the success of others as integral to our own individual success. Helping others within our spheres of influence to find new ways of improving the processes (and therefore the outcomes) of their work and their daily lives must be our central focus. In the new paradigm, educators will benchmark "best practices" of other educators' schools, as well as the worlds of business, governments, and other institutions, to discover "great ideas" we can use in our work, wherever those ideas may have originally sprung up. We will help students to benchmark their own efforts, so they can continuously improve their work by applying high standards to their own efforts and the efforts of other students in their spheres of influence. Again, this practice is what the Japanese mean by *kaizen*—a personal dedication to continuous improvement for yourself and those whose lives you touch.

We are in the business of human success—success for *all*—or we are surely in the wrong business altogether. If we're not in the business of building increasing capacities for success for ourselves, our colleagues, our students and their families, our communities and institutions, and all our customers, partners, and stakeholders, then the Quality philosophy and the Quality transformation certainly make no sense in our business.

Question #2: If we agree that our business is defined by the building of increasing capacities for human success, then what do we mean by *success* **in our business?** A tricky question, but an essential one. Success in our business must be viewed through a new understanding of the purpose of education. I have earlier suggested that education, in the new paradigm, will not be a delivery system for collections of fragmented information in the guise of curriculums. Instead, education will be a process that encourages continual progress through "the improvement of one's abilities, the expansion of one's interests, and the growth of one's character" (Bonstingl 1992, p. 67).

Xerox discovered that, when their customers and customers' customers succeed, Xerox succeeds. Likewise, when our colleagues, our students and their families, and our communities succeed with our help, we also succeed. Our definition of success must reflect a constant dedication to the exploration, discovery, and optimization of human potential in all its various forms, for everyone in our spheres of influence.

Successful leadership in this new paradigm is shown by the growth and development of people through encouragement, empowerment, and enabling, rather than by the temporary acquisition of artificial symbols of short-term gain through command, control, and compliance. Enlightened companies have come to realize that symbols such as numbers at the bottom of a profit-loss statement, or quarterly stock reports and dividends, are often poor instruments to evaluate past performance, current corporate health and growth, or potential for the future. We in education are coming to realize that symbols of student progress are all too often poor indicators of performance, potential, or the integrity of the student's personal systems of learning, growth, and development.

A more valid measure of the success of our work might be the degree to which people in a school or system develop ongoing processes that build metacognitive capacities and patterns of success in themselves and others. If we are serious about maximizing human potential in all its manifestations, all people must get better and better at knowing how they learn best, how they construct meaning from the sensory information they filter through their own life experience. People who recognize their own best ways of learning are often better able to help others to do the same. Such awareness is fundamental to one's *kaizen* journey of continuous improvement, and it is essential to the building of true communities of lifelong learners.

This realization suggests that we assess the hidden agendas inherent in the cultures of our schools and their systems and processes, including our curriculums. Open most curriculum guides and you will find page after page of answers. Our curriculums are, in reality, curriculums of answers. Answers to questions asked by teachers, textbooks, and tests— questions that, unfortunately, are almost never asked by our students. Why not rethink our idea of curriculums? Why not have curriculums of questions rather than curriculums of answers?

Based on his seven decades of living and five decades of teaching, Russell Ackoff has found that "learning begins with questions we cannot answer; it ends with questions we can" (Ackoff 1993, p. xii). If, as Deming observed, a "yearning for learning" is at the core of success in education and in life, why do we seem to accord so little time and value to the processes by which students, in collaboration with others (including ourselves), learn how to develop better and better questions in their ongoing quest to better understand themselves and our world.

Richard Feynman, the creative genius in physics whose work has been compared to that of Einstein, is said to have grown up in a family that never asked about grades, right answers on tests, and other often-artificial symbols of the temporary acquisition of data and information. Instead, when Feynman came home from school every day, his mother would ask, "Richard, what good questions did *you* ask in school today?"

Feynman's incredible capacities to connect far-flung ideas, to synthesize concepts—to understand how he processed data into information, information into knowledge, knowledge into understanding, and understanding into wisdom—are capacities that all students need to develop if they are to succeed. If they can equip themselves with a hunger to know more and more about how they and other people perceive, think, act, and learn, young people will naturally develop the unquenchable appetite for living and learning that is so fundamental to the exploration and development of what Howard Gardner (1993) calls their many "intelligences." And that, I believe, is what education must be all about.

Question #3: If we know what our business is, and if we know what we mean by *success* in our business, then how can we maximize success in our business? If, and only if, we can agree that our business is human success, and that success in our business is the maximization of human potential in all its various forms within ourselves, our colleagues, our students and their families, and our entire communities, then we can answer this question with a three-word response: the Quality Philosophy.

I believe it is well worth the time to contemplate these three essential questions before embarking on a Quality transformation for yourself and your organization. In our professional lives, this work is preliminary to the development of vision, values, and mission statements; effective strategic planning; and staff development. In our personal and family lives, as well, contemplating these three questions can provide new and sometimes surprising insights into why we do what we do.

6

Continuing the Journey

School leaders who are successfully applying Total Quality Management principles and practices to create Schools of Quality have
shared some helpful hints with me that you may find useful in
developing a customized culture of continuous improvement for your
school system:

• Learn as much as possible about Total Quality Management and
its applications to education. Before you try to make TQM a part of your
school system's everyday functioning, immerse yourself in the growing
body of literature on TQM as it applies to education as well as to the
business world. It may be helpful to attend TQM workshops and conferences, especially those presented by fellow educators who can effectively translate business-oriented TQM philosophies for use in
education organizations. You may also want to join organizations that
focus on the Quality Philosophy, such as ASCD's TQM-Education
Network.

Take time to discuss your Total Quality ideas with corporate leaders
in your community to get business perspectives on the Quality movement and local companies' continuous improvement processes. You
might also find it useful to bring in an education-focused consultant to
help you and other school leaders think through some of the thornier
issues you will confront when you begin the Total Quality transformation process. Learn how to use the Tools of TQM (see appendix 1),
understanding that these tools don't constitute the process of transfor-

mation, but they do provide ways of gathering and analyzing the necessary information for optimizing your systems and processes.

• Make a personal commitment to the Quality Philosophy and *kaizen* for yourself, your family, your schools, and your community. When you make your life a constant example of the journey toward Total Quality, you establish yourself as a role model for others in your community and schools. Demonstrate Quality leadership to staff members, associates, students, parents, and the entire community by "talking your walk and walking your talk." This behavior shows everyone that your new commitment to the Total Quality transformation process isn't simply another "flavor of the month," but rather a long-term philosophy of life. Those around you will begin to see the benefits of applying Total Quality principles to their own lives. When Total Quality permeates a community's thinking, the result is the establishment of a true "learning community" dedicated to the principle of *kaizen* in every aspect of life, including the work of young people and educators in all of the community's schools.

• Provide leadership by building networks of support for the transformation. Many school leaders have found it helpful to form a school-community Quality Council to determine needs and broad systemic goals, and to enlist the active support of all sectors of the community in accomplishing a Total Quality transformation. Representatives of all customer and supplier groups (internal and external) should be involved in the development of your schools' vision, mission, goals, principles, measures, and overall strategic plan. Crucial to the success of this process is partnership with local teacher and support staff organizations, who should be co-creators of the Total Quality transformation from the very beginning. Teachers, custodians, cafeteria workers, secretaries, administrators, parents, and students must be effectively represented if strong networks of support are to be created. The traditional fear-ridden Tayloresque environment of compliance, control, and command must be replaced by an environment of encouragement, nurturing, and collegiality.

• Build awareness of the Quality Philosophy throughout your organization and in your community. Use every opportunity to spread the news of the ongoing Total Quality transformation. In this neverending process, educators must teach young people and the entire community about the principles and practices of Total Quality, and support its implementation in all facets of community life. Your schools can, in time, become centers for modeling and teaching Quality to the entire community.

Instead of providing the media with symbolic numbers to demonstrate students' progress, you might provide local newspapers and TV stations with opportunities to observe and interview students who are demonstrating their real-life achievements in the schools and in the community. If your community has cable TV, use the public access channel to broadcast programs celebrating the ongoing processes of continuous improvement that are at the heart of your schools' and community's Total Quality transformation. It's much more effective for the people of the community to see with their own eyes the good things happening in their schools than to read published "box scores" comparing standardized test results of neighboring schools and school districts.

• Create a resource base to support the time and training necessary to make the transformation a long-term success. Make no mistake about it, a Total Quality culture in schools and communities cannot be created overnight. Effective, ongoing communication and teamwork will require investments of time (apart from classroom time) by teachers, administrators, and others. Training is an absolute *must*. Outside sources of information and facilitation will cost money and time, but we know that whatever expenditures are made at the front end of the transformation process will be repaid many times over as students become more successful in their school work, teachers and administrators work together more smoothly and effectively, and the community observes very real gains in student achievement.

• Assess the needs of customers and suppliers throughout your school and in your community. Who *are* your suppliers and customers, internal and external, primary and secondary? What are their needs, expressed and unspoken? How can your efforts result in processes and systems better designed to build Quality into the work everyone performs together, resulting in continuously improving customer satisfaction? Focus groups, surveys, brainstorming sessions, nominal group techniques, and other processes can help you gather data you will need to determine their needs and desires. Particular attention must be given to shifting demographic trends during the process of charting present and future needs. Work with childcare and social welfare agencies, lawmakers, and effective parenting groups to develop Total Quality community support environments conducive to the fullest development of your Schools of Quality. Extend your outreach efforts to all internal customers and suppliers within your organization. By building cross-disciplinary, multi-level teams of teachers, administrators, classified employees, parents, and students, you will be able to gather data that represent the widest possible range of customer/supplier perceptions and needs.

• Benchmark best practices inside and outside of education. Benchmarking is the process of scouting other organizations to identify the Total Quality systems and processes that your organization may want to emulate or adapt to your own local needs. How does your system compare with others? What could you, your customers, and your suppliers learn from other schools, communities, and organizations?

Remember when copying meant cheating? Today, in the cooperative learning classroom, as well as in institutional improvement processes, people are encouraged to search for standard bearers in their fields, learn from them, and apply their learnings to the continuous improvement of their own work and the work of their organizations. Using the TQM tools and techniques found in Appendix 1, you and your Quality Council may want to collect information from schools, companies, hospitals, and other organizations through on-site visits. Information can also be collected by phone and mail, through a search of the literature, and from outside consultants.

• Use the continuous improvement process on the processes and outcomes of your system. Start with a relatively small part of your system. Use the PDSA Cycle (or Juran's Spiral or the Experience Pattern Spiral) to delineate your continuous improvement process. Gather feedback information from customers and suppliers and use this feedback to constantly modify your systems and processes. This approach will be helpful for everyone throughout the school system, including students learning how to monitor their own educational processes, bus drivers trying to reduce the time variations of their bus runs, administrators seeking outside funding for school projects, teachers planning new initiatives to support greater student successes, and parents and other people of the community supporting their schools' continuous improvement processes. The applications of the continuous improvement process, as you will discover, are as endless as the Total Quality journey itself.

• Celebrate all successes, even small ones. The most successful Quality transformation efforts invariably recognize incremental improvements, especially by teams, and celebrate them in collaborative, noncompetitive environments. In the classroom, teachers and students share sincere celebrations of improvements in effort as well as results, with administrators and parents often joining in. Teacher teams are also recognized by their peers, administrators, and parents for their ongoing successes. Causes for celebrating improved efforts and achievements abound in Schools of Quality, limited only by the constraints of the imagination and by vestiges of Tayloresque management practices.

• Tie compatible existing educational philosophies and practices together under the Total Quality umbrella. Many school leaders have found that contemporary concepts and practices—site-based management, teaming, interdisciplinary courses, whole language, authentic assessment, mastery learning, and the effective schools research, to name a few—can easily be united under the Total Quality umbrella. When the Quality Philosophy and continuous improvement become unifying factors, these compatible components become part of an ongoing philosophy of commitment to improvement with roots that should grow deeper as time goes on.

• Make your journey to Total Quality a slow and steady process. The Quality transformation takes time. Avoid the temptation to plunge into it expecting your schools and community to achieve Total Quality status within a year or two. In most cases it takes at least two to three years of constant commitment and hard work to redesign suboptimizing systems and processes, and another two years to see tangible, long-lasting benefits. Spread the word to avoid the damaging effects of cynicism.

• Approach your Total Quality transformation with patience, forgiveness, and a helping hand. Total Quality is a journey, not a destination. To make the journey one that keeps getting better and better, everyone (especially school leaders) must be patient. The creation of Schools of Quality requires dramatic changes in the way people live and work. Change initially brings uncertainty, and oftentimes resentment. Old wounds may be reopened, and recriminations exchanged. The mixture of apprehension and exuberance with which many "front-line workers" initially greet their new decision-making powers often turns to frustration and cynicism when some of those decisions don't pan out. People who previously had little decision-making authority need time to learn how to use Quality tools, principles, and practices. Training in effective modes of active listening, partnership development discussion, and group problem-solving techniques will prove to be very solid investments in the long-term results of your Total Quality transformation.

Through the rough spots, it will be important to remember that the overarching reason for your efforts is to enable your own continuous growth and improvement and that of the people with whom you work and live. Getting better and better, day by day. *Kaizen.*

Reflecting upon his experiences implementing the widely known experiment in continuous improvement at Mt. Edgecumbe High School in Sitka, Alaska, Superintendent Larrae Rocheleau advised that a "general amnesty" be declared and respected by everyone in the system. Forgiveness of everybody's past offenses is crucial when developing a new, collaborative, team-focused Quality approach to replace outmoded authoritarian management modes.

In the years since the first edition of this book was published, hundreds of school leaders and policymakers who have initiated the Quality journey have generously shared with me their "Whatever you do, don't ever do this!" lists. Here is a brief compilation of their most often-cited mistakes, which might be called "Seven Stumbling Blocks on the Road to Quality." (There are many others! Let us know about your own discoveries for inclusion in subsequent editions of this book as well as in the newsletter *Quality Success Stories.*[1]) Any one of these seven practices is virtually guaranteed to put your Quality journey in dire jeopardy:

1. Failure to set clear, achievable expectations at the outset. "Without an aim, you have no system," Deming reminded us. Does everyone in your system know what the aim of your Quality transformation is? (An *aim* is more than a goal or objective; it is the direction of energy applied to the progressive realization of the ideal. Thus, an aim incorporates the entire process from the very beginning, including the attainment of goals and the system's growth from those achievements.)

Does every person know his or her role in contributing to the system's success over time? Leaders who want the Quality Philosophy to take root are careful to collect perspectives and data from all constituents on the system's strengths and areas for possible improvement; then they effectively communicate a clear vision to all the system's people, enlisting their active engagement in the long-term process of building new areas of competence upon the system's current strengths.

---

[1]*Quality Success Stories* is the newsletter of the ASCD Quality Education Network. For information on joining this international grassroots network, contact The Center for Schools of Quality, P.O. Box 810, Columbia, MD 21044 USA. Phone (410) 997-7555. E-mail: ASCDTQM@ aol.com

2. No constancy of purpose. Once the system's leadership establishes a Quality vision and aim for the organization, immediate follow-up must be provided. Otherwise, the system's people will naturally assume that the Quality Philosophy is just another in a long string of flavors of the month. Like the captain of a ship, the wise and effective leader provides constant direction to the system's crew, making sure that everyone is actively engaged in productive work with the same aim clearly in mind: that is, the building of greater and greater capacity within the system and its people over time.

All too often, when I am invited to visit a school system to give a talk or conduct a workshop on this topic, I find that people are wondering, *What does all of this have to do with **my** life?* We also discover that no follow-up plans have been announced (or even made, in some cases), no systemwide vision has been clearly communicated, and no clear aim has been conveyed to the people in the organization. Too bad! Missed opportunities are often not easily recoverable. The most successful Quality journeys are launched only after every member of the crew knows the purpose of the trip and the roles he or she will be expected to fill, and has developed a certain level of trust in the leader's ability to get the crew through the rough waters they may encounter along the way.

3. Fixing blame, applying coercion. Leaders falter in the Quality journey when they resort to coercion and blame whenever things begin to go wrong. "There will be a letter in your file tomorrow morning!" "Do this, or I'll call you on insubordination!" Glasser refers to such tactics as the "do it or we'll hurt you" school of coercive boss-management. In the long term, and often in the short run, these tactics backfire, making it difficult to reestablish a bond of trust and mutuality of effort toward a common aim.

When the vision is clear, and the course of the journey is set, and the aim of the system is known to all, leadership's job is to engage everyone's best energies in the process of removing institutional obstacles that stand in people's way. By focusing on this role, effective leaders empower and enable their crews to do their very best work on a constant basis.

4. Basing decisions on assumptions rather than on data. One of the most seemingly daunting aspects of the leader's journey in Quality is the need to constantly collect, interpret, and apply data in the decision-making process. It's much easier to simply operate on one's long-standing assumptions about the people, things, and situations that are familiar. It takes considerably more effort to constantly remind yourself to dig deeper into the issues, to take more time to seek out the opinions of others, to get insights from the people who use your work and from those whose work you use. The extra effort is well invested, however. The best "intuition" is often the end-result of years—even decades—of effective data collection and analysis. (See Appendix 1 for an example of "The Five Whys," a TQM tool useful in this practice.)

The leader's data collection process is greatly enhanced by what business consultant Tom Peters calls MBWA: Management By Walking Around. Ask the questions "How's it going?" and "How could we improve what we do around here, so that everybody will benefit?" and "Tell me what I could do to help you do an even better job than you are currently doing." All, of course, within a noncoercive and trustworthy organizational climate.

It's also important for school leaders to invest in educating all members of the school's learning community (including parents and the media) in the use of data. Much misunderstanding exists in this field, even among respected opinion leaders in education. For example, many believe that by comparing standardized test scores—say, the 8th grade scores this year with the 8th grade scores last year—they can find out something about the progress of the school, or at least about the 8th grade program. Such comparisons, unfortunately, do not tell us very much. Last year's class and this year's class are like apples and oranges, defying almost any meaningful comparisons. We would gain more by conducting an aggregated assessment of the same class over time: last year's 7th graders with this year's 8th graders, for instance. If the class has not changed its composition during the year, aggregate test scores can some-times be useful in the process of improving the school's teaching-learning systems.

5. Excluding key players from meaningful participation. From the very start of the Quality journey, leadership must actively enlist the support and participation of all key players and groups of stakeholders. To do otherwise is to invite trouble. Those who are not included will, legitimately, feel excluded. Hurt feelings often develop unnecessary polarization and suboptimization within the system. In one school district, for example, the central office administration and the school board decided to launch a Quality journey for the school district and its community, and they neglected to invite the teachers' organization to join the initial planning sessions. Their reasoning: Before bringing the teachers into the plans, leadership wanted to have all their "ducks in a row." Too bad. Their Quality journey was a dead duck, almost before it had a chance to get off the ground. This mistake, as it turned out, was not recoverable. To this day, tensions and suspicions still exist between the teachers and their administration and school board, in large measure built on this needless misunderstanding.

6. Failure to invest in training for leadership and for staff. Before launching a systemwide Quality journey, leaders must invest the time and energy required to learn about the Quality Philosophy—its theory, practice, benefits, and challenges. This philosophy can appear deceptively simple; it is not. As in everything else in life, it is helpful to have a certain degree of comfort and intimacy with the ideas one seeks to teach to others. Ongoing staff development and leadership development are absolute necessities at every stage of the Quality journey.

World-class, leading-edge companies spend between 5 and 10 percent of their annual budgets on staff development. On average, American schools spend less than one-half of one percent of their budgets on staff development. Time constraints are another stumbling block. Businesses can often simply shut down the shop and provide training for their people. Schools cannot afford such a luxury. And yet this point is clear: Without effective training on a constant basis, your Quality journey will be in grave danger. Link forces with others in the community who have seen the benefits of staff development in their own companies' and organizations' Quality journeys. These people can be formidable allies in the struggle to coalesce the scarce resources necessary for effective Quality training. Consider alternative time-use models, including block scheduling, to better provide the time required for staff and leaders to plan and learn together.

7. Failure to walk the talk. Trust is built upon people's perceptions of their leaders' trustworthiness. To be most effective, the Quality Philosophy must transcend the workplace. When people see leaders acting one way at work and another (contradictory) way at home and in the community, the preconditions for trust are easily eroded. With the erosion of trust comes the incapacity to lead any kind of Quality transformation process.

Those leaders who *are* Quality receive their people's tacit permission to lead the Quality journey; other leaders, including those who attempt to mandate TQM without modeling it, may find that their powers are effectively circumscribed, allowing them a more limited (and often less palatable) set of leadership style options. The "need" for coercive boss-management is often born of such circumstances.

Here is a commonly cited example: When you invest in staff development, make sure you are at the workshops from start to finish. Everybody knows that if the top dog is present and participating (as a learner among learners), the workshop is important. The leader's absence for any part of the workshop sends a clear message: "This is not worth my time." Others may think: *If this isn't worthy of our leader's time, then it's not worthy of our time. Why, then, do we have to sit through this?* Too bad. A golden opportunity needlessly squandered. More important, it provides yet another avoidable reason for the organization's people to become more cynical and to feel justified in believing they are victims of the system. Effective leadership requires more than just walking your talk. Your people must know intuitively that anything you would ask of them, you would gladly do yourself, including taking personal risks to advance the common cause of your Quality community of learners.

Schools of Quality, as well as other Total Quality organizations, are places where it is safe to take wise risks, okay to fail occasionally on the way to success. Some have suggested that, throughout life, *failure* is a counterproductive mental construct. There is no such thing as failure. There is, instead, only ongoing personal development, which of necessity must include successes and areas for continual improvement. What we call "failures" are a natural part of life's journey. Encourage and support the creation and expression of new ideas, from the classroom to the principal's office to the school board conference room, and into the larger community.

A story, perhaps apocryphal, is told of Thomas Edison. One day, he was asked by a reporter, "Mr. Edison, why did you fail more than 10,000 times before you finally invented the light bulb?" Edison, never known for his humility, responded, "My dear sir, you are mistaken. I did not fail 10,000 times before I invented the light bulb. The invention of the light bulb happened to have been a 10,000-step process!"

As you begin your Quality journey, let me share with you one of my favorite thoughts on this topic, which first appeared as a full-page ad in the *Wall Street journal* more than a decade ago. Reprinted on the next page in its entirety, it is entitled "Don't Be Afraid To Fail."

Don't Be Afraid To Fail

You've failed
many times,
although you may not
remember.
You fell down
the first time
you tried to walk.
You almost drowned
the first time
you tried to
swim, didn't you?
Did you hit the
ball the first time
you swung a bat?
Heavy hitters,
the ones who hit the
most home runs,
also strike
out a lot.
R. H. Macy
failed several
times before his
store in New York
caught on.
English novelist
John Creasy got
753 rejection slips
before he published
564 books.
Babe Ruth struck out
1,330 times,
but he also hit
714 home runs.
Don't worry about
failure.
Worry about
chances you miss
when you don't
even try.

Reprinted through courtesy of Harry J. Gray, Harry Gray Associates

7

Quality as a Way of Life

Quality is a way of being. It is a lifelong journey of the spirit, body, and mind that permeates all aspects of one's life. Quality grows first inside our hearts and souls. Then it grows in our relationships with others. Whenever Quality becomes the essence of our being when we are alone and when we are with others, it naturally thrives in and defines our families and other groups to which we belong.

Ultimately, Quality becomes the essence of our schools, our workplaces, and our communities, and then of our society, and eventually of the global village of which we are a part. When the number of Quality-oriented people reaches a critical mass at a particular level, the Quality Philosophy naturally becomes the way of being at that level.

Quality cannot be delegated, Deming reminded us. Quality must be led and managed from the top. Everyone is at the top of something. What are you at the top of, and what can you do right now, today, to begin your Quality journey or to advance it within yourself and with those in your spheres of influence?[1]

People of Quality know that the Quality Philosophy adds immeasurable richness and value to their lives. Only by becoming dedicated practitioners of Quality in all aspects of their being will they advance the quality of life within themselves and within their environments.

---

[1]My appreciation to Don Stewart, president of Savannah Tech, for sharing this insight with me.

The daily practice of Quality focuses on five essential disciplines, which I call my Five Personal Practices of Quality[2]:

1. Leadership. The first Personal Practice of Quality is Leadership with gratitude and integrity. Management can be practiced without gratitude and integrity, but true leadership requires both. The word *gratitude* comes from the Latin root *gratia,* meaning "thanks" or "appreciation." The effective leader has a healthy appreciation for himself or herself and demonstrates sincere personal appreciation for others, publicly and behind the scenes. *Gratia* is also the root of our English words *grace* and *graciousness.* The most effective leaders create in the work environment a state of *grace,* or forgiveness, in which people know that it is safe to take wise risks and to fail occasionally on the road to continuous improvement.

The Quality leader establishes a gracious and hospitable place for people to work together. The exercise of true hospitality requires extending a warm welcome to everyone, even those whose company you may not particularly enjoy. This practice certainly holds true in the workplace. And, for those who wish to live their Quality journey with the greatest possible integrity, the disciplined exercise of graciousness and hospitality extends to every facet of life—at home with their families, on the road in their cars, in the shopping malls, in their places of worship—a commitment that permeates every waking moment.

The personal practice of Leadership also requires integrity. The word *integrity* comes from a root word meaning "one" or "whole." Leaders of integrity work to unite in common purpose and action those people who are in their spheres of influence. They strive for unity and wholeness within themselves and in their dealings with others. In their derivations, the words *whole* and *heal* are closely related, and the most effective leaders are those who are truly healers—healers first of self, then of others, and of the environments in which they work and live. Leaders who seek to impose the Quality Philosophy upon others without first consistently and overtly exemplifying the Philosophy in their own lives set themselves up for frustration and failure, and they unwittingly create the circumstances in which cynicism, divisiveness, and mediocrity thrive.

---

[2]These practices are related to my Four Pillars of Quality, described in Chapter 4.

Here are three questions to guide your personal practice of Leadership:

- How can I best lead my own life with gratitude, creating a gracious and hospitable environment for myself and others?
- How can I best lead my own life with integrity, working toward wholeness and healing within myself and in my relationships with others?
- How can I best work with others to create fulfilling, ongoing relationships grounded in the Quality Philosophy?

2. Partnership is my second Personal Practice of Quality. True Partnership is not about winning and losing. Partnership requires us to reject the impulse to win at our partner's expense. Whenever we seek an advantage over our partner, a part of us loses in the bargain. "Who wants to be married to a loser?" Deming mused. Indeed, who wants to work with a loser? Be friends or lovers with a loser? Who wants their kids to be losers?

Whenever we cause another to lose so we can win, we betray our partnership. Likewise, whenever we establish win-win relationships with our partner, we run the risk of unconsciously setting our partnership against the external world. *If both of us win, then who shall lose?* may become the unstated assumption. When things go wrong in win-win relationships, the tendency is to think: *Well, I'll continue to let my partner win while I'm winning too, but I'm going to make sure he (or she) doesn't win more than I'm winning!*

Partnership focuses on the essential questions: *What are the two of us really about together, here in this moment? In whose service are we called to be here?* This essential focus on the Personal Practice of Partnership creates the physical-mental-spiritual space in which possibilities can be created, suffering can be reduced, and life can best be served.[3]

Here are three questions to guide your personal practice of Partnership:

- How can I best work with others to build our capacity to improve the processes and products of our efforts?
- How can I best communicate my needs to those people whose work I use?

---

[3]I am indebted to Professor John Greenfelder Sullivan of Elon College for suggesting these essential aims of Partnership in the truest sense.

• How can I best communicate with those people who use my work, so I can meet (and even anticipate) their needs on a constant basis?[4]

3. Systems Thinking and Systems Action is the third Personal Practice of Quality. People who practice this daily discipline are alert to the surrounding world. Systems thinkers pay attention to the ways in which people and things are interconnected, and work to understand the many levels on which these relationships are built. They seek to identify cause-and-effect relationships, with the understanding that the most proximate, observable causes may not be as directly related in time and place as circumstances suggest.

The daily practice of Quality requires us to acknowledge that 85 percent or more of the things that go wrong in any system result from the way we set up and perpetuate our patterns of interaction. It asks us to be patient with one another, to lend a helping hand rather than to point an accusing finger, remembering that systems most often fail people before people fail within their systems. There is more disability in our systems than there is disability in the people within our systems, more ability in our collective efforts than in our solitary efforts. As Deming was fond of saying, "Don't fix blame. Work together to fix the system. That's where your problems are."

Here are three questions to guide your practice of Systems Thinking and Systems Action:

• How can I best discover how people and things are really connected?

• How can I best demonstrate my dedication to fixing the system, rather than fixing blame, with a deep understanding that systems most often fail their people before people fail within their systems?

• How can I best create positive changes in my spheres of influence, so everyone—including myself—can succeed and be happier?

4. Process Orientation. The fourth Personal Practice of Quality is Process Orientation. This way of thinking and acting was described earlier in Chapter 3: "Learning a New Way to Swim." The process-oriented person knows that it is vitally important to have an aim. "Without an aim, you have no system," Deming reminded us. And, without a system, you have no way to chart your progress. An aim is therefore

---

[4]Questions 2 and 3: The term *work* is understood here to mean the processes and products of effort expended at all levels of functioning, not only at one's place of work, but also at home and in the community.

necessary, but an aim by itself is insufficient. If the aim is to be realized, it must be supported by appropriately devised processes within optimizing systems. "By what method? By what method?" Deming hammered home the point: How are you going to get where you want to go?

Blind insistence on the attainment of goals without the necessary investment in systems and processes required to bring about those results is naive at best, deceitful and polemical at worst. In any case, it is ultimately counterproductive, resulting in frustration, bitterness, apathy, and burnout. Practitioners of Quality, by comparison, know that every high-quality product is the result of constancy of purpose and action, applied to the continuous improvement of processes and systems designed to bring about specific results. They know that the integrity of end-products depends on the integrity of processes and systems. If you want Quality at the end, you must front-load Quality at the beginning and maintain it throughout the process.

Here are two questions to guide your personal practice of Process Orientation:

• How can I best understand the meaning of my life and its significance in changing the course of events within myself, in my family, in my community and larger society, and in my world?

• How can I intentionally infuse Quality into every moment of my life, so my life will have greater integrity and meaning in all of its processes and products?

5. Constant Dedication to Continuous Improvement. My fifth Personal Practice of Quality is a disciplined, constant focus on Continuous Improvement for oneself and those who are in one's spheres of influence, through the exercise of leadership, partnership, systems thinking and systems action, and process orientation. This focus is the essence of the Quality journey.

Here are two questions to guide your personal practice of Continuous Improvement:

• How can I best use my time and talents to improve myself every day?

• How can I best help others in my spheres of influence—at home, at work, and in the community—to do the same?

I firmly believe that life offers each of us only two options. The first option is to be forever a victim, convinced that your ideas don't count, that no one really listens to you or appreciates you, that nothing you do will ultimately make a difference, that you are the reflexive object of other people's actions upon you. If you affirm your victimhood in the presence of others, you will always have company (particularly in the faculty lounge).

The second option is to be a real-life champion, actively working to build a better life for everyone—a true Quality world—by bringing people together in pursuit of good ideas that make it possible for everyone to experience greater and greater success and happiness. Each of us must make the choice: mediocrity and victimhood, or championship and Quality? Which will it be?

Former Texas governor Ann Richards tells a story that illustrates this choice. She calls it her "Drop the Rock" story, and it goes something like this. Mary is drowning in the sea. A boat comes alongside her, and people reach out their arms to help her. "Mary!" they shout, "Grab onto our hands and we'll help you climb on board!" Mary responds, "I'm drowning, I'm drowning! I can't reach that far!" Mary sinks lower and lower in the water.

"Mary!" one of the lifesavers shouts, "We can help you to be saved, but first you have to *drop the rock!*"

"Rock? *What* rock?" Mary shouts back.

"The one around your neck!" the lifesaver replies.

Mary feels around her neck. She touches something hard and heavy, and says, "Oh, you mean *this*? Why, this has been with me for years! I couldn't let *this* go!"

"Mary! Drop the rock, or you'll surely drown!" cries the lifesaver. "Hurry, Mary! There's not much time left!"

End of story. Will Mary drop the rock and save herself from going under? Or will she cling desperately to the very thing that's defeating her best efforts? Will Mary choose the comfort of victimhood and certain demise? Or will she choose to own her own life and discard that which, little by little, pulls her down?

Are there any rocks around your own neck? Around the neck of your family? Your school? Your community? What will you choose to do about those rocks around your neck, beginning right now, today?

Through the daily practice of Quality, we become role models for others to observe and emulate. Our life experiences become richer and more fulfilling. Relationships become healthier and more substantial. Our organizations become more effective and humane.

When Quality becomes a way of life, we rise to a state of being characterized by what Deming called a natural "pride and joy" in the processes and products of our lives through a yearning for learning that is lifelong, life-wide, and life-deep. This is a journey without end, an invitation to participate in a lifelong adventure to seek out the very best that life has to offer!

APPENDIX 1
Tools for the Transformation

In the process of transforming their organizations into Total Quality learning organizations, leaders in business, education, and other spheres have found it helpful to use TQM tools and techniques to better perceive, collect, analyze, and understand relevant data. This appendix takes a brief look at the TQM tools that are most useful for educators in their schools' journey of continuous improvement.

First, a word of caution and clarification. As Marshall Sashkin and Kenneth Kiser (1993) have warned: "The tools are not TQM." Tools and techniques, they stress, are useful but "not sufficient for 'TQM.' When made the focus of TQM, tools and techniques can even prevent the organization from taking the additional steps needed for TQM. In this way, an overemphasis on tools, in the mistaken belief that the tools are TQM, can lead the organization in the opposite direction, away from an organizational commitment to quality."

The Seven Traditional Tools

We will start with the Seven Traditional Tools, as they are known by practitioners of TQM. An application for schools is provided for each tool.

Tool 1: The Flow Chart
Detailed Flow Chart

The Flow Chart is a diagram of the steps in a process, shown in their natural sequence. By showing how a process works in practice, potential difficulties can be identified and short-circuited, resulting in the creation of a new, improved process. This tool is useful in the process of thinking through a new process before it is implemented so that potential pitfalls can be more easily avoided.

In the following example (see page 52), a state school boards association used this Detailed Flow Chart to diagram the sequence of a strategic vision and planning process. This chart shows the developmental stages of a school district's vision, mission statement, goals and objectives, strategies, and action plan.

The process of creating this flow chart resulted in better communication and greater buy-in by all persons involved in the process of school transformation. Because all of the steps in this process were clear from the outset, the statewide transformation began with a much better chance for long-term success.

69

DETAILED FLOW CHART

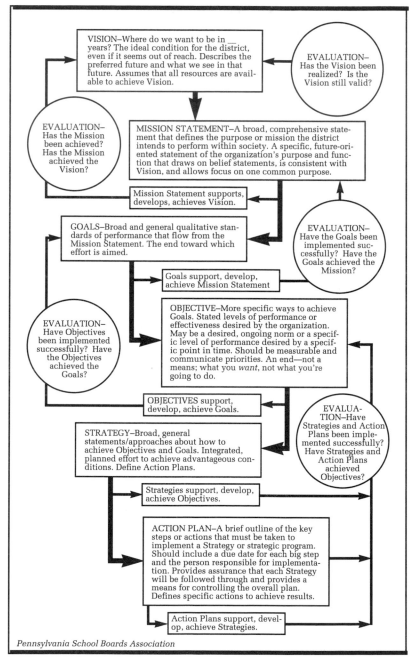

VISION–Where do we want to be in __ years? The ideal condition for the district, even if it seems out of reach. Describes the preferred future and what we see in that future. Assumes that all resources are available to achieve Vision.

EVALUATION– Has the Vision been realized? Is the Vision still valid?

EVALUATION– Has the Mission been achieved? Has the Mission achieved the Vision?

MISSION STATEMENT–A broad, comprehensive statement that defines the purpose or mission the district intends to perform within society. A specific, future-oriented statement of the organization's purpose and function that draws on belief statements, is consistent with Vision, and allows focus on one common purpose.

Mission Statement supports, develops, achieves Vision.

GOALS–Broad and general qualitative standards of performance that flow from the Mission Statement. The end toward which effort is aimed.

EVALUATION– Have the Goals been implemented successfully? Have the Goals achieved the Mission?

Goals support, develop, achieve Mission Statement

OBJECTIVE–More specific ways to achieve Goals. Stated levels of performance or effectiveness desired by the organization. May be a desired, ongoing norm or a specific level of performance desired by a specific point in time. Should be measurable and communicate priorities. An end—not a means; what you *want*, not what you're going to do.

EVALUATION– Have Objectives been implemented successfully? Have the Objectives achieved the Goals?

OBJECTIVES support, develop, achieve Goals.

EVALUA-TION–Have Strategies and Action Plans been implemented successfully? Have Strategies and Action Plans achieved Objectives?

STRATEGY–Broad, general statements/approaches about how to achieve Objectives and Goals. Integrated, planned effort to achieve advantageous conditions. Define Action Plans.

Strategies support, develop, achieve Objectives.

ACTION PLAN–A brief outline of the key steps or actions that must be taken to implement a Strategy or strategic program. Should include a due date for each big step and the person responsible for implementation. Provides assurance that each Strategy will be followed through and provides a means for controlling the overall plan. Defines specific actions to achieve results.

Action Plans support, develop, achieve Strategies.

Pennsylvania School Boards Association

Here is another example of a Detailed Flow Chart, showing the steps in a school's attendance process. An administration-teacher team used this tool to understand the existing process so their improvement efforts could be based upon a full understanding of current practices.

DETAILED FLOW CHART

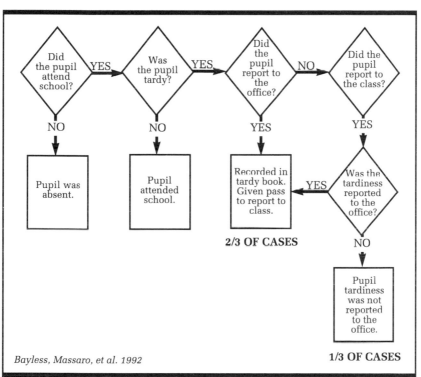

Bayless, Massaro, et al. 1992

Top-Down Flow Chart

Another type of flow chart, the Top-Down Flow Chart, has many applications to education. Students can use it to analyze their learning processes, identifying those steps that need more time and effort, or perhaps a different approach. Interdisciplinary teacher teams can use the flow chart to map out a new interactive process for cross-disciplinary instruction. School boards can use it to plan construction of new school facilities or the implementation of new policies.

In the following example, a team of teachers and school leaders used a Top-Down Flow Chart to identify the steps they needed to take together in order to implement a Total Quality transformation in their school district.

TOP-DOWN FLOW CHART

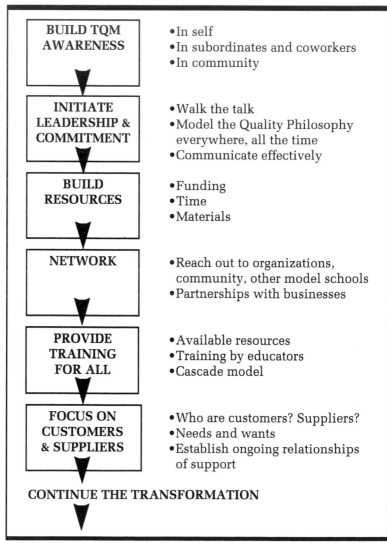

BUILD TQM AWARENESS	• In self • In subordinates and coworkers • In community
INITIATE LEADERSHIP & COMMITMENT	• Walk the talk • Model the Quality Philosophy everywhere, all the time • Communicate effectively
BUILD RESOURCES	• Funding • Time • Materials
NETWORK	• Reach out to organizations, community, other model schools • Partnerships with businesses
PROVIDE TRAINING FOR ALL	• Available resources • Training by educators • Cascade model
FOCUS ON CUSTOMERS & SUPPLIERS	• Who are customers? Suppliers? • Needs and wants • Establish ongoing relationships of support

CONTINUE THE TRANSFORMATION

The process of creating this Flow Chart *as a team* resulted in greater buy-in from everyone involved in the transformation process. Because all of the team members felt a part of the process from the outset, the transformation began with a much better chance for long-term success.[1]

Tool 2: The Fishbone Diagram

This tool, called the Fishbone because of its shape, is also known as the Cause-and-Effect diagram or the Ishikawa diagram, after its creator, Kaoru Ishikawa. The Fishbone, shown on p. 74, is helpful in determining the root causes and effects within an organization's processes and systems. It is a modification of the "process arrow" diagram discussed in Chapter 3.

The Fishbone can be used to identify factors in the process responsible for an existing problem or to plan a process more effectively, so that inputs result in the desired outcomes.

To use the Fishbone to uncover the causes of an existing problem, first write the outcome problem or condition you want to study in the "head" of the fish, on the right. Then, on the big "bones" of the fish, list the major factors possibly responsible for the outcome. On the little bones, write the factors that possibly contribute to, or modify, the major factors that ultimately lead to the current outcome.

Here is an example of the Fishbone used to analyze a school problem: bus runs arriving late. In this example, despite everyone's best intentions and efforts, several bus runs had been arriving late every day at a particular school. This resulted in some students coming into their 1st period classes as much as twenty minutes late. The school administration created a team consisting of parents, students, bus drivers, the transportation supervisor, and the school's vice principal to study the problem and come up with possible solutions. To collect and analyze data relevant to this dilemma, they used a Fishbone diagram. The diagram on p. 74 shows what it looked like after the team had filled it in.

Notice that, after listing the factors they considered most significant on the "skeleton," the team circled those factors having the strongest impact on the problem: the length of some bus routes, the age of the buses, and the number of students and stops on each bus route. The team found that some bus routes required the pick-up of nearly twice the

---

[1]See Peter Scholtes, et al., *The Team Handbook* for more about Detailed and Top-Down Flow Charts.

COMPLETED FISHBONE DIAGRAM

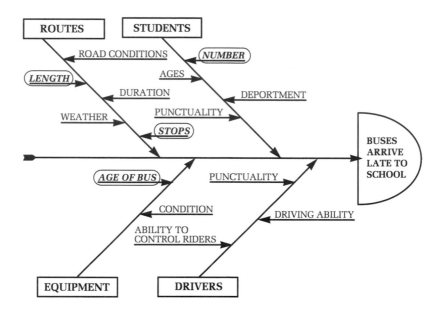

number of students as other routes, and that those bus runs took an average of 60 percent longer than the shortest bus runs. Also, the oldest buses were being used for the longer routes.

Using the data they collected, the team petitioned the school board for several new bus runs. Once the new runs were established, all of the bus runs arrived at school well before the beginning of first period. Problem solved!

The Fishbone can also be used to plan an improvement process. When a Quality Circle S-Team of students used the Fishbone to plan ways of improving their school work, they came up with the data in the completed Fishbone Diagram on p. 75.

The student team determined that a more attractive school environment, improved relationships with teachers, increased support by parents and families, and some extra assistance from members of their S-Team would help them improve their learning processes, energizing them to make better grades and to achieve the "greatest possible success" in their classes. Based upon the data, the student team organized other

Completed Fishbone Diagram

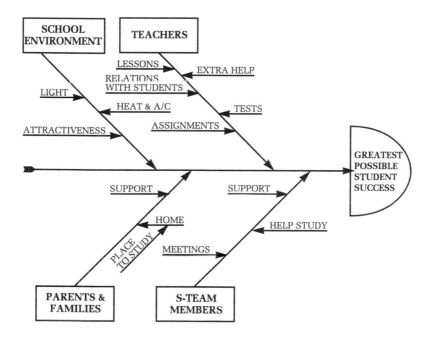

students into a committee to clean up and improve the appearance of the school campus; they began to work more closely with their teachers to improve the effectiveness of their interactions inside and outside of the classroom; and they talked with their family members to create times and spaces within their homes that would be more conducive to effective studying. The students also agreed to meet once a week in their S-Teams to give additional help and support to one other in their own continuous improvement and learning processes. This plan resulted in better grades for all of the team's members, enhanced pride and joy in their work, and a greater feeling of belonging and shared caring.

Tool 3: Pareto Chart

The Pareto Chart is named after the 19th century Italian economist Vilfredo Pareto, whose research was used by Joseph Juran in formulating what he called the Pareto Principle: Relatively few *vital* factors (as little as 20%) are responsible for the vast majority (as much as 80%) of all problems in any process or system. The lesson of the Pareto Principle is this: Analyze your information carefully, so you can identify the *vital few* factors that require attention first and foremost. The Pareto Chart is a bar chart in which factors in a process are shown in descending order of importance or frequency of occurrence.

The following Pareto Chart was used by an administration-teacher team to study the types of student disruptions in their classes. Finding that the vast majority of all disruption problems came from students talking in class, they focused their attention on this factor, instituting student training and more interactive teaching that takes into account students' learning styles and capitalizes on students' desire to communicate with each other in class. This strategy resulted in a dramatic decrease in class disruptions.

PARETO CHART

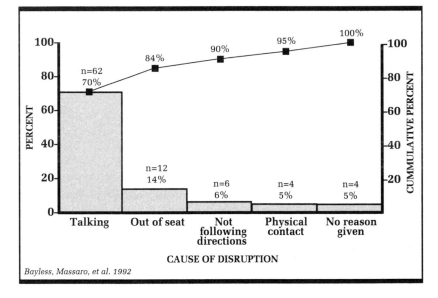

Bayless, Massaro, et al. 1992

Tool 4: The Scatter Diagram

The Scatter Diagram is a tool used to analyze the correlation between two variables. It can be used to identify possible cause-effect relationships between factors in a process. In the Scatter Diagram, the measures of one factor are shown on the horizontal axis, while measures of the other factor are shown on the vertical axis. If there is a positive correlation between the two factors, indicating a possible cause-effect relationship, the direction of the cluster of points will show a directional design from lower left to upper right. Any other pattern indicates the absence of a positive correlation between the two factors, thus putting into doubt the existence of a cause-effect relationship.

In the following example, a student was taught how to use the Scatter Diagram to analyze the relationship between hours spent studying and test grades.

By using the Scatter Diagram, the student was convinced that there is a positive correlation between study time and test grades.

SCATTER DIAGRAM

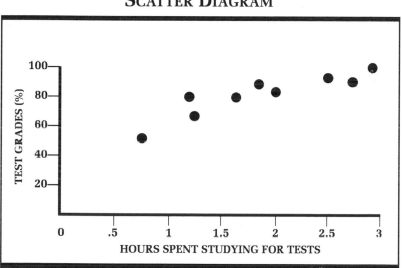

Tool 5: The PDSA Cycle

The Plan-Do-Study-Act Cycle invented by Walter Shewhart and developed by W. Edwards Deming is a useful tool for carrying on a continuous improvement process. The PDSA Cycle is a model of the way people learn, so it can help us analyze and improve the processes we use in getting a job done.

Students can be taught to use the PDSA Cycle to better understand the systemic nature of their own learning processes. Here is an example of a PDSA Cycle developed by a student.

In this example, the student plans how to approach the work of the new unit (in the "Plan" step). Then the student does the work of the unit (the "Do" step), taking notes, doing the required and suggested reading, participating in class, doing assignments including the unit project, and taking the unit test. All the while, the student keeps a journal, reflecting on the processes chosen to accomplish all the tasks of the unit.

At the end of the unit, the student and teacher collaboratively study the processes they used to accomplish the goals of the unit (the "Study" step). Using the student's journal and all of the work done by the student, they examine what went right and what should be improved in their work together in the next unit.

Then, in the "Act" step, the student and teacher use what they have learned in this process to improve the ways the next unit is done. Thus, the PDSA Cycle becomes a vehicle for teachers and students to continu-

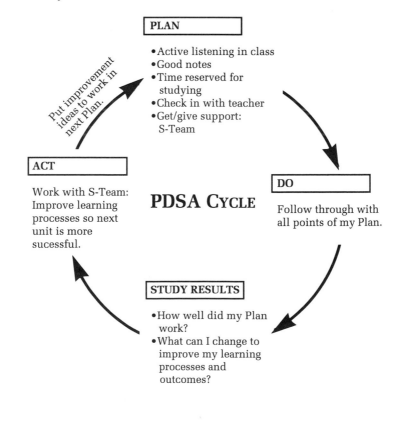

PDSA CYCLE

PLAN
- Active listening in class
- Good notes
- Time reserved for studying
- Check in with teacher
- Get/give support: S-Team

DO
Follow through with all points of my Plan.

STUDY RESULTS
- How well did my Plan work?
- What can I change to improve my learning processes and outcomes?

ACT
Work with S-Team: Improve learning processes so next unit is more sucessful.

Put improvement ideas to work in next Plan.

ously improve their collaborative efforts to create better and better ways of interacting with each other, toward greater and greater successes.

The PDSA Cycle is one of the most versatile Quality tools. It can be used to study and improve virtually any process, from conducting effective and efficient faculty meetings and school board sessions to planning field trips, from conducting community and customer surveys to attracting more parents and business people to support the work of the school.

Tool 6: The Histogram

The Histogram is a bar chart representation of the spread or dispersion of variable data. Histograms tend to show a natural distribution toward the center prior to intervention. An example for schools is the bell curve, showing a natural clustering of grades in a pretest before the beginning of the unit (or instructional intervention) as shown here.

HISTOGRAM

Please note: It is neither natural nor desirable to have grades *at the unit's end* conform to the normal distribution of a bell curve. If the pretest does not show a normal distribution, further analysis is needed to determine whether there are special causes or common causes of variation—helpful data in determining how best to teach the unit.

Tool 7: The Control Chart

The Control Chart (sometimes called the Statistical Control Chart) is used to display graphically the variation in an ongoing process. This tool, invented by Walter Shewhart, began the statistical process control movement, which was the precursor of the Total Quality Management movement in industry and education.

The Control Chart has a horizontal axis for tracking time and a vertical axis for tracking the system or process under consideration. If the process goes outside the upper or lower control limits, it is considered "out of statistical control." In such cases, the system should be adjusted to bring the process back into control.

Let's say the optimum temperature for a school building is 72 degrees, and that the upper and lower control limits of your heating system have been plotted at 76 and 68 degrees. This is the normal variation, within the constraints of your present system. To decrease the 11 point spread, your system must be changed. If the temperature goes outside that range, you need to determine whether the reason is a special cause of variation, or a common cause, and take appropriate actions.

The procedure for using a Control Chart is rather sophisticated, and may require further research and the services of a professional statistician.

CONTROL CHART

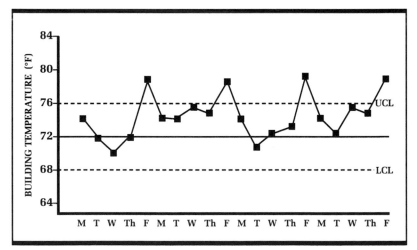

Newer Tools

In addition to the Seven Traditional Tools, newer TQM tools for planning and problem solving are being developed as new needs arise. Here are a few of the newer tools and some of their applications to education.

Tool 8: The Affinity Diagram

The Affinity Diagram method, developed by Kawakita Jiro, is a simple categorization process, putting together chosen factors that have a natural link with one another. The Affinity Diagram is often a preliminary step before using the Fishbone Diagram. Take another look at the first Fishbone diagram (p. 74). This is an Affinity Diagram that might have been designed before that Fishbone was created.

Notice that the major headings under the title of the Affinity Diagram provide the context for the factors written in the Fishbone diagram.

AFFINITY DIAGRAM

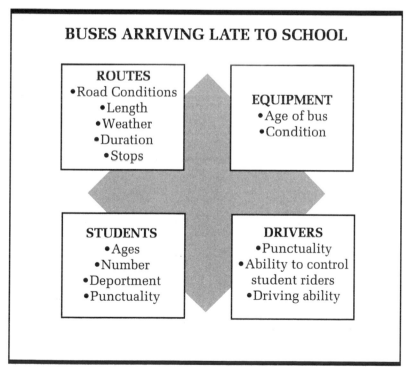

BUSES ARRIVING LATE TO SCHOOL

ROUTES
- Road Conditions
- Length
- Weather
- Duration
- Stops

EQUIPMENT
- Age of bus
- Condition

STUDENTS
- Ages
- Number
- Deportment
- Punctuality

DRIVERS
- Punctuality
- Ability to control student riders
- Driving ability

Tool 9: The Force Field

The Force Field, or Restraining Forces and Driving Forces, developed by Kurt Lewin (1948), provides a method for identifying the factors opposing change and those pushing for change. By weighing the factors on both sides, and effectively counterbalancing the negative factors, it is possible to develop an action plan with a great chance of succeeding in the long run.

Here is a Force Field showing some restrainers and drivers in the implementation of a districtwide Total Quality transformation process.

FORCE FIELD

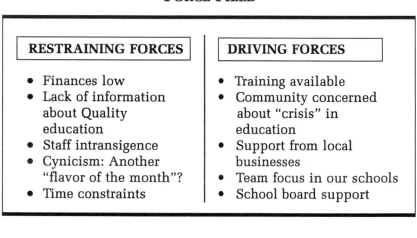

RESTRAINING FORCES	DRIVING FORCES
• Finances low	• Training available
• Lack of information about Quality education	• Community concerned about "crisis" in education
• Staff intransigence	• Support from local businesses
• Cynicism: Another "flavor of the month"?	• Team focus in our schools
• Time constraints	• School board support

Tool 10: The Five Whys

Uncovering the real reasons behind a problem often requires a process that goes deeper than simply answering the question "Why?" A Japanese tradition suggests that only after answering that question five times will the true causes of a problem begin to emerge. Here is an example:

1. Why didn't you do your homework last night?
   I didn't have time to do my homework.
2. Why didn't you have time to do your homework?
   I had other things I had to do.
3. Why did you have other things to do?
   I had to be with my little brother.
4. Why did you have to be with your little brother?
   Because there was no one else at home.
5. Why was there no one else at home?
   Because my parents went to a party and my little brother started throwing up right after they left. I had to take care of him until my parents got home after midnight, and then I was too tired to do my homework. If it's okay with you, I'll hand it in tomorrow.

Tool 11: Cross-Impact Matrix

A Cross-Impact Matrix (or CIM) is a tool used to analyze the impact, or effect, of a certain factor upon a specific area of consequence. The simplest kind of CIM is a table of horizontal and vertical columns. At the beginning of each horizontal row, one of a set of related factors is given. At the top of each column, specific areas of consequence are listed. Each factor in a row is matched with each area of consequence listed in a column, one at a time. The matching of factors and areas of consequence raises the question: What impact do factors and areas of consequence have on each other?

Here is an example of a CIM designed to help students consider the various possible effects of drug use. As students fill in the matrix, they become more and more aware of the wide scope of personal repercussions if they choose to abuse drugs.

CROSS-IMPACT MATRIX

MAKING PERSONAL DECISONS ABOUT DRUG USE				
	Relations with my Family	Relations with my Friends	Impact on my Body and Mind	Impact on my Future
Alcohol	*My parents would be disappointed if I used alcohol.*	*Some of my friends want me to use it, others do not.*	*I could get addicted to alcohol and get cancer of the liver.*	*I could get arrested for underage use and hurt my future plans.*
Tobacco				
Marijuana				
Ecstacy				

Adapted from *Introduction to the Social Sciences*, 4th edition, Prentice Hall (1996), by John Jay Bonstingl.

Tool 12: The Decision Wheel

The Decision Wheel (sometimes called the Ripple Effect Diagram) is a tool for thinking through the probable effect of actions taken. The decision or action to be studied is written in the center bubble. The actual or probable effect of the central action is written in the four bubbles surrounding the central action in the middle bubble. Then, in the bubbles of the second circle, the actual and probable effects of the first circle's effects are described. The Decision Wheel shows graphically the effects, often unintended, of our actions.

Here is a Decision Wheel completed by students whose S-Team decided to collect canned food for their community's soup kitchen. Through their work with this Decision Wheel, they gained a fuller appreciation of the systemic ripple effects of their efforts.

DECISION WHEEL

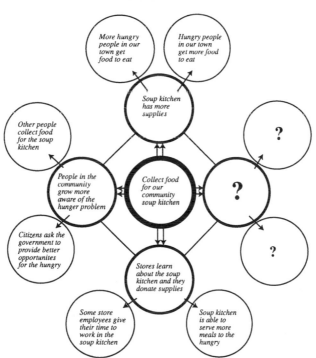

Adapted from *Introduction to the Social Sciences*, 4th edition, Prentice Hall (1996), by John Jay Bonstingl.

Tool 13: The Checksheet

Checksheets are a well-known device for recording data. Necessary information about the characteristics of a process or a product can be recorded by simply making a check mark. Checksheets are particularly useful in spotting omissions that may be detrimental to the success of a process.

Here is an example of a checksheet that might be used in the process of preparing for a faculty meeting.

CHECKSHEET

CHECKLIST FOR FACULTY MEETING

ITEM	YES	NO
1. Agenda Handouts	√	
2. Business cards for all faculty members	√	
3. Get well card for R.J.	√	
4. Articles on TQM in education	√	
5. New Board Policy	√	
6. Inservice courses	√	

These are only a few of the many TQM tools and techniques available for use in the Total Quality transformation process. Brainstorming, nominal group techniques, benchmarking, customer/supplier surveys and questionnaires, and other methods of getting, arranging, and analyzing data can also be helpful in your Quality journey.

Once again, it is good to remember that however useful these tools may be in the process of continuous improvement, they are not the transformative process itself, and should not be considered the heart and soul of the process. To place such importance on the tools is to potentially deny the importance of the people who are at the heart of every transformative process, including that of your Quality journey.

APPENDIX 2
The Four Pillars of Schools of Quality: Roles of Stakeholder-Participants

Pillar #1: A Customer-Supplier Focus

Policy-makers	Customers of school leaders and those they serve, including students, teachers, administrators, parents and families, and other stakeholders in the community's schools.
	Suppliers of policies designed to facilitate the optimization of the entire system, permitting students and teachers—as the school's front-line workers—to maximize everyone's potentials through a constant focus on process-oriented continuous improvement.
School Leaders	Customers of families who send their children to the school, of vendors who supply the school with necessities, and of state and federal agencies that create legal contexts for schools.
	Suppliers of effective fear-free environments and policies that benefit all contributors to the continuous improvement of the school and its people.
Teachers	Customers of families who send their children to school, of administration and school board policies, and of other teachers who work with the same students.
	Suppliers of supportive mentoring to students, helping them in a wide variety of ways to continuously improve their character, competency, and compassion.

PILLAR – 1A

Students	Customers of efforts by teachers, administrators, and support staff who provide environments and services conducive to the students' continuous improvement.
	Suppliers of consistent effort toward their own continuous improvement and that of others at school, at home, and in the community.
Parents and Families	Customers of the school's total effort on behalf of their children.
	Suppliers of pre- and post-natal physical and psychological support to help maximize their children's opportunities for growth and development of innate intelligences. Suppliers of consistent personal involvement in support of the school and its people.
Business People	Customers of the school's total effort toward the maximization of successes by students and teachers in their work together.
	Suppliers of financial and in-kind support, and opportunities for teachers, students, and others in the school and community to learn about continuous improvement from a business point of view.
Community Members	Customers of the school in terms of continuing opportunities to learn, to contribute to community improvement, and to leave a legacy for coming generations.
	Suppliers of financial and psychological support for the continuous improvement of the school and its people. Good schools need more than tax monies. They need the active support of everyone, even citizens without school-age children.

PILLAR – 1B

Appendix 2—continued
The Four Pillars of Schools of Quality:
Roles of Stakeholder-Participants

Pillar #2: Constant Dedication to Continuous Improvement (*Kaizen*)

Policy-makers	Demonstrate constant dedication to continuous improvement of self and others at home, at work, and in the community. Create policies to build fear-free learning environments, systems, and processes most conducive to *kaizen* and the creation of a "yearning for learning" among students, teachers, school leaders, and all the people of the school and community.
School Leaders	Demonstrate constant dedication to continuous improvement of self and others at home, at work, and in the community. Help policymakers to create policies that support fear-free learning environments, systems, and processes most conducive to *kaizen* and the creation of a "yearning for learning" among students, teachers, school leaders, and all the people of the school and community.
Teachers	Demonstrate constant dedication to continuous improvement of self and others at home, at school, and in the community. Create fear-free classroom environments and learning processes that help students identify and constantly develop their wide range of innate abilities. Show young people how to learn and share with others, helping everyone to grow and improve every day. Help students create within themselves an unquenchable "yearning for learning," developing the tools required to learn and grow.

PILLAR – 2A

Students	Demonstrate constant dedication to continuous improvement of self and others at home, at school, and in the community. Develop the courage to improve character, competence, and compassion more and more fully every day. Seek and maximize opportunities for lifelong and life-wide learning, in and out of school, for self and others.
Parents and Families	Demonstrate constant dedication to continuous improvement of self and others at home, at work, and in the community. Provide children and other family members with real-life role models who love to learn and who build active relationships of unconditional love and mutual respect for everyone in the family, knowing that such relationships are the fertile ground of continuous growth and improvement of character, competence, and compassion.
Business People	Demonstrate constant dedication to continuous improvement of self and others at home, at work, and in the community. At work, help build a fear-free company culture based upon trust, respect, and mutual dedication to everyone's continuing growth and development. Know that growth of the bottom line is less important than the growth of the one true resource that makes a consistently healthy bottom line possible: people, especially the young. Develop a Total Quality culture in which the school's graduates can continue to learn, grow, and nourish themselves and others as employers, employees, and coworkers.
Community Members	Demonstrate constant dedication to continuous improvement of self and others at home, at work, and in the community, particularly in full support of the school and its people. This dedication is shown by vocal and financial support to fully fund school efforts and a communitywide dedication to lifelong and life-wide *kaizen* learning for all.

PILLAR – 2B

APPENDIX 2—continued
The Four Pillars of Schools of Quality:
Roles of Stakeholder-Participants

Pillar #3: A Process/Systems Approach

Policy-makers	Create policies that design quality into the system and its processes from the very beginning. Work from the start with the educators who will implement the policies, learning from their experience at the front lines.
School Leaders	Build quality into the system and its many interlinking processes. See things gone wrong as opportunities to fix the system rather than to fix blame on individuals. The health of relationships within the system must be given priority over short-term symbols of the system's outcomes.
Teachers	Build quality into the system of teaching and learning. Create learning opportunities that connect with students' other real-life experience—the larger life-system of which schooling is one of many processes. As integral elements of the students' personal learning systems, teachers work with students to constantly fine-tune their ongoing work processes so that successive units of study can be learned with greater and greater mastery.

PILLAR – 3A

Students	Build quality into personal learning systems. Focus on connections between what school teaches and what other real-life experiences teach. Concentrate on ways of improving character, competence, and compassion in self and others, which results in continuous improvement in a wide range of efforts.
Parents and Families	Help students and teachers build quality into their work together by emphasizing children's learning processes, not just grades and other short-term indicators of learning programs. Use voice and vote to support systems and processes of continuous learning for everyone in the community—especially young people. Combine efforts with other people in the system to create synergistic progress.
Business People	Build quality into systems and processes. Offer insights to the school and its people sharing successes and providing support to employees. Stress the systemic nature of continuous improvement in the world of business, and foster such efforts in the school. Help develop partnerships with the school and its people, for everyone's long-term benefit.
Community Members	Support the school's systemic and process-oriented transformations in teaching and learning. Know that simplistic numerical symbols of students' performances are not adequate indicators of the health of learning systems and processes within the school. Communicate this knowledge to the media.

PILLAR – 3B

APPENDIX 2—continued
The Four Pillars of Schools of Quality: Roles of Stakeholder-Participants

Pillar #4: Strong and Consistent Total Quality Leadership

Policy-makers	Create policies that encourage a constant dedication to Total Quality by everyone within the system, and by everyone impacted by the system.
School Leaders	"Quality cannot be delegated," taught W. Edwards Deming. Only management can initiate organizational cultures of Quality. Workers, acting alone, cannot do it. School leaders must "talk their walk and walk their talk" in everything they do if Total Quality is to eventually permeate all aspects of the school and its community. There are no quick fixes or magic bullets. TQM is not a flavor of the month; it must be developed through teamwork, with deliberation, over the span of years.
Teachers	
Students	Everyone in the school and the community must be supportive of the changes school leaders must make
Parents and Families	in the process of transforming schools into Schools of Quality. Changes bring pleasures and pains.
Business People	Everyone must be ready to experience both, over time, with patience and dedication, if Total Quality is to
Community Members	inform the deep culture of the school and its community.

PILLAR – 4

APPENDIX 3
Deming's Fourteen Points Applied to Companies and Schools

The following represents the author's interpretation of The Fourteen Points developed by Dr. W. Edwards Deming, internationally renowned authority in the field of statistical quality control.

POINT	COMPANIES	SCHOOLS
1 Create constancy of purpose for improvement of product and service.	Company must focus on staying in business and providing jobs through research, innovation, and continual improvement of products and services. Maximization of profits is less important than this focus.	School must focus on helping students to maximize their own potentials through continuous improvement of teachers' and students' work together. Maximization of test scores and assessment symbols is less important than the progress inherent in the continuous learning process of each student.
2 Adopt the new philosophy.	Company leaders must adopt and fully support the new philosophy of continuous improvement through the empowerment of front-line workers. Cynical application of the new philosophy, with the sole intent of improving the bottom line, destroys interpersonal trust, which is essential to success.	School leaders must adopt and fully support the new philosophy of continuous improvement through greater empowerment of teacher-student teams. Cynical application of the new philosophy for the sole intent of improving districtwide test scores destroys interpersonal trust, which is essential to success.

APPENDIX 3—*continued*

POINT	COMPANIES	SCHOOLS
3 Cease dependence on mass inspection.	Reliance on assessment of the final product at the end of the production line is inherently wasteful. Substandard products must be trashed and replaced, or reworked to specifications. The right time for assessment is at every point in the entire production process. The best people for assessment are the customers and the people who are on the front lines of production.	Reliance on tests as the major means of assessment of student production is inherently wasteful and often neither reliable nor authentic. It is too late at the end of the unit to assess students' progress if the goal is to maximize their productivity. Tests and other indicators of student learning should be given as diagnostic and prescriptive instruments throughout the learning process. Learning is best shown by students' performance, applying information and skills to real-life challenges. Students must be taught how to assess their own work and progress if they are to take ownership of their own educational processes.
4 End the practice of doing business on price tag alone.	Work closely with suppliers to build relationships of trust and collaboration. Don't allow only suppliers' prices to determine your company's use of their materials and services. Work together to maximize efficiency and productivity.	Build relationships of trust and collaboration within the school, and between the school and the community. Everyone's roles as supplier and customer must be recognized and honored. Work together whenever possible to maximize the potentials of students, teachers, administrators, and the community.

APPENDIX 3—*continued*

POINT	COMPANIES	SCHOOLS
5 Improve constantly and forever the system of production and service.	Company management must create and maintain the context in which the workers are empowered to make continuous progress in product and service improvement, while they minimize waste and inefficiency.	School administrators must create and maintain the context in which teachers are empowered to make continuous progress in the quality of their learning and other aspects of personal development, while they learn valuable lessons from (temporary) failures.
6 Institute programs of training.	Company leaders must institute programs of training for new workers. Effective training programs show workers how to set goals, how to work more effectively, and how to assess the quality of their own work.	School leaders must institute programs of training for new employees unfamiliar with the specific culture and expectations of the school. Effective training programs show new teachers how to set goals, how to teach effectively, and how to assess the quality of their work with students. Teachers must also institute programs in which students learn how to set learning goals, how to be more effective in their school work, and how to assess the quality of their own work. Teachers should show students by attitude and actions what a good *learner* is all about. (Educators learn how to be educators from the modeling they receive as students.)

APPENDIX 3—*continued*

POINT	COMPANIES	SCHOOLS
7 Institute leadership.	Leading consists of working with others as coach and mentor so that the organizational context in which improvement is valued and encouraged can be maximized by front-line workers. Leading is helping, not threatening or punishing.	School leadership consists of working with teachers, parents, students, and members of the community as coach and mentor so that the organizational context in which all students' growth and improvement is valued and encouraged can be maximized by teachers and students, parents, and community members who support the common effort. Leading is helping, not threatening or punishing.
8 Drive out fear.	Fear is counterproductive, especially in the long term. Fear breeds distrust, cynicism, divisiveness, apathy, and disaffection, all of which lead to declines in productivity. Institutional changes must reflect shared power, shared responsibilities, and shared rewards.	Fear is as counterproductive in school as it is in the workplace. Fear is destructive of the school culture and everything good that is intended to take place within it. Institutional changes must reflect shared power, shared responsibilities, and shared rewards.
9 Break down barriers between staff areas.	Company productivity is enhanced when departments view themselves as partners in progress, and work together to maximize their potentials. Create cross-departmental and multi-level quality teams to break down role and status barriers to productivity.	Teacher and student productivity is enhanced when departments combine talents to create more integrated opportunities for learning and discovery. Create cross-departmental and multi-level quality teams to break down role and status barriers to productivity.

APPENDIX 3—*continued*

POINT	COMPANIES	SCHOOLS
10 Eliminate slogans, exhortations, and targets for the workforce.	Workers who are in charge of their own production will create slogans, exhortations, and targets that are more meaningful than those imposed from above, as long as power, responsibility, and rewards are equitably distributed. When company expectations are not met, fix the system instead of fixing blame on individuals.	Teachers, students, administrators, families, and community members may collectively arrive at slogans and exhortations to improve their work together, as long as power, responsibility, and rewards are equitably distributed. When educational goals are not met, fix the system instead of fixing blame on individuals.
11 Eliminate numerical quotas.	Quotas are numerical symbols that do not reflect the quality of the productive process, the integrity and health of the system, or long-term indicators of successes and failures. In fact, "hitting the numbers" as a short-term bottom-line solution to worker or company challenges is often useless or counterproductive in the long run.	Assignments and tests that focus attention on numerical or letter symbols of learning and production often do not fully reflect the quality of student progress and performance. When the grade becomes the bottom-line product, short-term gains replace student investment in long-term learning, and this may prove counter-productive in the long run.
12 Remove barriers to pride and joy of workmanship.	Workers generally want to do good work and feel pride in it. Companies must dedicate themselves to removing the systemic causes of worker failure through close collaborative efforts.	Teachers and students generally want to do good work and feel pride in it. Schools must dedicate themselves to removing the systemic causes of teacher and student failure through close collaborative efforts.

Appendix 3—continued

POINT	COMPANIES	SCHOOLS
13 Institute a vigorous program of education and retraining.	Company management and the entire workforce require continuous learning programs if the company is to be on the leading edge and maximize customer satisfaction. Company people benefit from encouragement to enrich their education by exploring ideas and interests beyond the boundaries of their professional and personal worlds.	All of the school's people benefit from encouragement to enrich their education by exploring ideas and interests beyond the boundaries of their professional and personal worlds. Administrators, teachers, and students require continuous learning programs if the school is to be on the leading edge and maximize customer satisfaction.
14 Take action to accomplish the transformation.	Company people at all levels must put this new philosophy into action so it becomes embedded into the deep structure and culture of the organization. Workers alone cannot put the plan into effect. Constant top-level dedication to full implementation must be supported by a critical mass of company people to implement the plan and make it stick.	School personnel at all levels (including students) must put this new philosophy into action so it becomes embedded into the deep structure and culture of the school. Teachers and students alone cannot put the plan into effect. Constant top-level dedication to full implementation must be supported by a critical mass of school and community people to implement the plan and make it stick.

APPENDIX 4
The Quality Paradigm Shift in Education:
From Teaching and Testing to
Continuous Learning and Improvement

Old Paradigm of Teaching and Testing	New Paradigm of Continuous Learning and Improvement
Success is artificially limited to a few "winners." All others are made to consider themselves and their work as mediocre or inferior.	Unlimited, continuous improvement and successes are the objectives of schooling.
Competition-based.	Cooperation-based.
Lessons are linear, consecutive segments of one-way communication.	Learning is like a spiral with offshoots, with energy directed toward continuous improvement. Assessments are used for diagnostic and prescriptive purposes.
Product-oriented; focused solely on results, without acknowledgment of their short-term nature. Grades and rankings are important in themselves.	Process-oriented. Goals are important, but the process of getting to the goal is at least as significant. Assessments are used for diagnostic and prescriptive purposes.
Life, including schooling, is only worthwhile if you reach goals. The process has little or no intrinsic merit, and must be abbreviated whenever possible so the goals can be reached sooner.	Life is a journey, and has intrinsic merit if lived with a zest for life, love, and learning. Developing a "yearning for learning" is most important of all.
The system and its processes don't matter as long as the ends are achieved.	The integrity and health of the system, its processes, and its people must be maintained, or the system will be suboptimized, and will eventually fail.
Work is a task, not intended to bring joy to the worker.	Work should be challenging, invigorating, and meaningful. Everyone in the school should take pride and joy in the products and processes of the work.

Old Paradigm

New Paradigm

School as a place where teaching is done to (at) students. Students are passive, teachers are active.

School is a true community of learners in which administrators, teachers, and students learn how to get better and better at the work they do together, so that everyone succeeds optimally.

Teachers are isolated from each other by time and space.

Teachers work together to build success with each other and with a manageable number of students in a cohort group.

Administration is viewed as the teachers' natural adversary (perhaps as the enemy).

Administrators are viewed as teammates and partners in removing the obstacles to student and teacher successes.

Teachers are viewed as the students' natural adversaries (perhaps as enemies).

Teachers are viewed as teammates and partners in removing obstacles to continuous success.

Tayloresque factory model: Rule by compliance, control, command. Authoritarian, hierarchical. Management based upon fear.

New model: Lead by helping and by providing vision and support toward the aim and mission of the school, making it possible for teachers and students to take greater and greater pride in their work together and to have joy in the processes and products of continuous improvement. (In Japan this is called *kaizen*.)

Centralized control over resources, curriculum, teaching methods, length of class periods, school day, school year, and so on.

Site-based management of resources, curriculum, methods, time considerations, and so on.

Single-discipline instruction.

Multi- and cross-discipline learning.

Old Paradigm

External validation of truth and the "one right answer" for every question asked by teacher, text, and test.

Testing as primary means of assessing the results of the learning process.

Instruction is set up to generate (right) answers.

Teachers are expected to know everything about their subjects. They give students data and information; students memorize it, then promptly forget most of it. Competency demonstrated in exams is short-lived, though this is not reflected in the durable nature of the grades representing that supposed competency.

Parents are outsiders, often made to feel unwelcome, even if unintentionally.

New Paradigm

External and internal truths discovered through students' and teacher's questioning together.

Testing, when appropriate, to help modify (improve) the teaching/learning process. Other modes include process portfolios, exhibitions, student-led teacher-parent conferences, performances, and so on.

Instruction is set up to generate better and better questions, followed by student inquiry into some of the areas of those questions. Student performances demonstrate improved understanding of the nature of the questions and some of the ways they might be solved.

Teachers are experts in their field. But more importantly, they are the most enthusiastic and dedicated learners in the classroom. Students learn from teachers, other students, community, and other sources, and incorporate those learnings into their lives, applying their insights as appropriate to real-life challenges.

Parents are partners, suppliers, and customers. They are an integral part of the student's progress from the very beginning through the end of the schooling process.

Old Paradigm

Businesses are sometimes welcomed to "adopt" a school; kept at arm's length.

People of the community are not encouraged to take part in the life of the school, or in the education of the community's young people. Not encouraged to have pride in the community schools.

Ultimate goal: Students as products of the school.

New Paradigm

Businesses are invited to become partners (secondary suppliers and customers) in the students' continuous progress, not for direct commercial gain.

People of the community are brought into the school and made welcome, encouraged to contribute time and talents to the betterment of their school and their community's children.

Ultimate goal: Students as their own products, continually improving, expanding their interests, improving their abilities, and developing character— getting better and better every day and helping others to do the same.

APPENDIX 5
The Educational Impact of the Quality Philosophy in Schools:
A Report of The Conference Board of Canada[1]

The Conference Board of Canada conducted a study of schools that infused the Quality Philosophy (TQM) into their functioning at all levels. This study concludes that Schools of Quality enjoy these benefits:

• Students develop positive attitudes about themselves as learners. They learn more, their SAT scores improve, and drop-out rates and discipline problems are greatly reduced as school becomes a more positive force in their lives.

• The classroom becomes more interactive, with less lecture time and better use of student teamwork. Students learn to apply Quality tools and techniques to successfully meet challenges.

• New ways of learning—including peer coaching, self-evaluation, and peer evaluation—encourage students to take fuller advantage of their opportunities to learn and grow.

• The shift is toward results-focused learning, with great emphasis on process, systems, and relationships as Quality principles and practices are used in instruction and curriculum design.

• Administration becomes more effective. Counterproductive irritants for teachers, students, parents, and others are eliminated. As a result, the system's effectiveness dramatically improves.

• Staff morale improves. Labor-management relations are smoother. Better planning and decision making lead to continuous improvement and greater satisfaction.

---

[1]Adapted from *Total Quality in the Schools: Preliminary Findings* (Ottawa: The Conference Board of Canada, 1993).

APPENDIX 6
The SCANS Report[1]

In 1991 the Office of the U.S. Secretary of Labor published the findings of a national blue-ribbon panel composed of educators, business people, union representatives, and government officials who had been studying these two questions: "What competencies will young people need to develop, in order to survive and thrive in the workplace of the future?" and "How can we best prepare young people today for their role in the workforce of the future?"

The work of this panel, known as the Secretary's Commission on Achieving Necessary Skills (or the SCANS Commission), has significant implications for educators dedicated to building the Quality Philosophy into the work we do in our communities' schools and businesses. The Executive Summary of The SCANS Report is reproduced here in slightly abridged form:

Executive Summary

The Secretary's Commission on Achieving Necessary Skills (SCANS) was asked to examine the demands of the workplace and whether our young people are capable of meeting those demands.

Specifically, the Commission was to advise the Secretary on the level of skills required to enter employment. In carrying out this charge, the Commission was asked to:

- Define the skills needed for employment;
- Propose acceptable levels of proficiency;
- Suggest effective ways to assess proficiency; and
- Develop a dissemination strategy for the nation's schools, businesses, and homes.

This report results from our discussions and meetings with business owners, public employers, unions, and workers and supervisors in shops, plants, and stores. It builds on the work of six special panels we established to examine all manner of jobs from manufacturing to government employment. We also commissioned researchers to conduct lengthy interviews with workers in a wide range of jobs.

---

[1] *What Work Requires of Schools: A SCANS Report for America 2000* (Washington, D.C.: U.S. Department of Labor, 1991), pp. xv-xxii.

The message to us was universal: good jobs will increasingly depend on people who can put knowledge to work. What we found was disturbing: more than half our young people leave school without the knowledge or foundation required to find and hold a good job. These young people will pay a very high price. They face the bleak prospects of dead-end work interrupted only by periods of unemployment.

Two conditions that arose in the last quarter of the 20th Century have changed the terms for our young people's entry into the world of work: the globalization of commerce and industry and the explosive growth of technology on the job. These developments have barely been reflected in how we prepare young people for work or in how many of our workplaces are organized. Schools need to do a better job and so do employers. Students and workers must work smarter. Unless they do, neither our schools, our students, nor our businesses can prosper.

SCANS research verifies that what we call *workplace know-how* defines effective job performance today. This know-how has two elements: *competencies* and a *foundation*. This report identifies five competencies and a three-part foundation of skills and personal qualities that lie at the heart of job-performance (see Figures 1 and 2). These eight requirements are essential preparation for all students, both those going directly to work and those planning further education. Thus, the competencies and the foundation should be taught and understood in an integrated fashion that reflects the workplace *contexts* in which they are applied.

We believe, after examining the findings of cognitive science, that the most effective way of learning skills is "in context," placing learning objectives within a real environment rather than insisting that students first learn in the abstract what they will be expected to apply.

The five SCANS competencies span the chasm between school and the workplace. Because they are needed in workplaces dedicated to excellence, they are hallmarks of today's expert worker. And they lie behind the quality of every product and service offered on today's market.

The competencies differ from a person's technical knowledge. For example, both accountants and engineers manage resources, information, systems, and technology. They require competence in these areas even though building a bridge has little to do with balancing a set of books. But in each profession, the competencies are at least as important as technical expertise. The members of the Commission believe these competencies are applicable from the shop floor to the executive suite.

FIGURE 1
Five Competencies

Resources: Identifies, organizes, plans, and allocates resources

A. *Time*—Selects goal-relevant activities, ranks them, allocates time, and prepares and follows schedules

B. *Money*—Uses or prepares budgets, makes forecasts, keeps records, and makes adjustments to meet objectives

C. *Material and Facilities*—Acquires, stores, allocates, and uses materials or space efficiently

D. *Human Resources*—Assesses skills and distributes work accordingly, evaluates performance and provides feedback

Interpersonal: Works with others

A. *Participates as Member of a Team*—contributes to group effort

B. *Teaches Others New Skills*

C. *Serves Clients/Customers*—works to satisfy customers' expectations

D. *Exercises Leadership*—communicates ideas to justify position, persuades and convinces others, responsibly challenges existing procedures and policies

E. *Negotiates*—works toward agreements involving exchange of resources, resolves divergent interests

F. *Works with Diversity*—works well with men and women from diverse backgrounds

Information: Acquires and uses information

A. *Acquires and Evaluates Information*

B. *Organizes and Maintains Information*

C. *Interprets and Communicates Information*

D. *Uses Computers to Process Information*

Systems: Understands complex inter-relationships

A. *Understands Systems*—knows how social, organizational, and technological systems work and operates effectively with them

B. *Monitors and Corrects Performance*—distinguishes trends, predicts impacts on system operations, diagnoses deviations in systems' performance and corrects malfunctions

C. *Improves or Designs Systems*—suggests modifications to existing systems and develops new or alternative systems to improve performance

Technology: Works with a variety of technologies

A. *Selects Technology*—chooses procedures, tools or equipment including computers and related technologies

B. *Applies Technology to Task*—understands overall intent and proper procedures for setup and operation of equipment

C. *Maintains and Troubleshoots Equipment*—Prevents, identifies, or solves problems with equipment, including computers and other technologies

In the broadest sense, the competencies represent the attributes that today's high-performance employer seeks in tomorrow's employee.

. . . [W]ork involves a complex interplay among the five competencies we have identified and the three elements of the foundation—the **basic skills**, higher order **thinking skills**, and diligent application of **personal qualities.**

. . . [T]omorrow's career ladders require even the basic skills—the old 3 Rs—to take on a new meaning. First, all employees will have to **read** well enough to understand and interpret diagrams, directories, correspondence, manuals, records, charts, graphs, tables, and specifications. Without the ability to read a diverse set of materials, workers cannot locate the descriptive and quantitative information needed to make decisions or to recommend courses of action. What do these reading requirements mean on the job? They might involve:

- interpreting blueprints and materials catalogues;
- dealing with letters and written policy on complaints;
- reading patients' medical records and medication instructions; and
- reading the text of technical manuals from equipment vendors.

At the same time, most jobs will call for **writing skills** to prepare correspondence, instructions, charts, graphs, and proposals, in order to make requests, explain, illustrate, and convince. On the job this might require:

- writing memoranda to justify resources or explain plans;
- preparing instructions for operating simple machines;
- developing a narrative to explain graphs or tables; and
- drafting suggested modifications in company procedures.

Mathematics and **computational skills** will also be essential. Virtually all employees will be required to maintain records, estimate results, use spreadsheets, or apply statistical process controls as they negotiate, identify trends, or suggest new courses of action. Most of us will not leave our mathematics behind us in school. Instead, we will find ourselves using it on the job, for example, to:

- reconcile differences between inventory and financial records;
- estimate discounts on the spot while negotiating sales;
- use spreadsheet programs to monitor expenditures;
- employ statistical process control procedures to check quality; and
- project resource needs over the next planning period.

FIGURE 2
A Three-part Foundation

Basic Skills: Reads, writes, performs arithmetic and mathematical operations, listens and speaks

A. *Reading*—locates, understands, and interprets written information in prose and in documents such as manuals, graphs, and schedules
B. *Writing*—communicates thoughts, ideas, information, and messages in writing; and creates documents such as letters, directions, manuals, reports, graphs, and flow charts
C. *Arithmetic/Mathematics*—performs basic computations and approaches practical problems by choosing appropriately from a variety of mathematical techniques
D. *Listening*—receives, attends to, interprets, and responds to verbal messages and other cues
E. *Speaking*—organizes ideas and communicates orally

Thinking Skills: Thinks creatively, makes decisions, solves problems, visualizes, knows how to learn, and reasons

A. *Creative Thinking*—generates new ideas
B. *Decision Making*—specifies goals and constraints, generates alternatives, considers risks, and evaluates and chooses best alternative
C. *Problem Solving*—recognizes problems and devises and implements plan of action
D. *Seeing Things in the Mind's Eye*—organizes, and processes symbols, pictures, graphs, objects, and other information
E. *Knowing How to Learn*—uses efficient learning techniques to acquire and apply new knowledge and skills
F. *Reasoning*—discovers a rule or principle underlying the relationship between two or more objects and applies it when solving a problem

Personal Qualities: Displays responsibility, self-esteem, sociability, self-management, and integrity and honesty

A. *Responsibility*—exerts a high level of effort and perseveres towards goal attainment
B. *Self-Esteem*—believes in own self-worth and maintains a positive view of self
C. *Sociability*—demonstrates understanding, friendliness, adaptability, empathy, and politeness in group settings
D. *Self-Management*—assesses self accurately, sets personal goals, monitors progress, and exhibits self-control
E. *Integrity/Honesty*—chooses ethical courses of action

Finally, very few of us will work totally by ourselves. More and more, work involves listening carefully to clients and co-workers and clearly articulating one's own point of view. Today's worker has to **listen** and **speak** well enough to explain schedules and procedures, communicate with customers, work in teams, understand customer concerns, describe complex systems and procedures, probe for hidden meanings, teach others, and solve problems. On the job, these skills may translate readily into:

- training new workers or explaining new schedules to a work team;
- describing plans to supervisors or clients;
- questioning customers to diagnose malfunctions; and
- answering questions from customers about post-sales service.

SCANS estimates that less than half of all young adults have achieved these reading and writing minimums; even fewer can handle the mathematics; and, schools today only indirectly address listening and speaking skills.

Defining the minimum levels of proficiency in the SCANS competencies is also a crucial part of the Commission's task. It requires judgments about the learning possible in yet-to-be-designed schools. It also requires imagining what the workplaces of the year 2000 could and should look like.

Our work on these required levels of proficiency is not complete. We have examined less than a third of the jobs we intend to research. We also wish to hear what others think of our initial efforts. Figure 3 is illustrative of our initial estimates of work-ready levels of proficiency in the five competencies. Proficiency in each competency requires proficiency in the foundation. The contexts displayed come from more extensive scenarios contained in our report. The point we wish to make is that young people leaving school should have both a sufficient foundation and level of understanding of the competencies to exhibit performances like those illustrated.

The minimums we propose will define what makes a young person ready for work at entry levels on career ladders. They represent neither the first nor last step in a process of life-long learning. Instead, the minimums will be a second step in a progression of skills acquisition. For example, consider scheduling time, part of the SCANS resources competency. A young student (at the preparatory stage) might be expected to make a schedule for him or herself. Being *work-ready* would require making a schedule for others. At the extreme, a specialist might develop schedules for an airline (see Figure 4). . . .

FIGURE 3
Know-How:
Work-Ready Level of Proficiency

Competence	Example of Level
RESOURCES	Develop cost estimates and write proposals to justify the expense of replacing kitchen equipment. Develop schedule for equipment delivery to avoid closing restaurant. Read construction blueprints and manufacturers' installation requirements to place and install equipment in the kitchen.*
INTERPERSONAL	Participate in team training and problem-solving session with multicultural staff of waiters and waitresses. Focus on upcoming Saturday night when local club has reserved restaurant after midnight for party. Three people cannot work and team has to address the staffing problem and prepare for handling possible complaints about prices, food quality, or service.*
INFORMATION	Analyze statistical control charts to monitor error rate. Develop, with other team members, a way to bring performance in production line up to that of best practice in competing plants.**
SYSTEMS	As part of information analysis above, analyze painting system and suggest how improvements can be made to minimize system downtime and improve paint finish.**
TECHNOLOGY	Evaluate three new paint spray guns from the point of view of costs, health and safety, and speed. Vendors describe performance with charts and written specifications. Call vendors' representatives to clarify claims and seek the names of others using their equipment. Call and interview references before preparing a report on the spray guns and making a presentation to management.**

*Competence as demonstrated in a service sector application.
**Competence as demonstrated in a manufacturing sector application.

FIGURE 4
Progress In Acquiring Skills

Proficiency Level	Performance Benchmark
PREPARATORY	Scheduling oneself
WORK-READY	Scheduling small work team
INTERMEDIATE	Scheduling a production line or substantial construction project
ADVANCED	Developing roll-out schedule for new product or production plant
SPECIALIST	Develop algorithm for scheduling airline

The President of the United States has encouraged all of us to become revolutionaries in the cause of education. For over 200 years Americans have worked to make education part of their national vision, indispensable to democracy and to individual freedom. For at least the last 40 years, we have worked to further the ideal of equity—for minority Americans, for the disabled, and for immigrants. With that work still incomplete, we are called to still another revolution—to create an entire people trained to think and equipped with the know-how to make their knowledge productive.

This new revolution is no less exciting or challenging than those we have already completed. Nor is its outcome more certain. All that is certain is that we must begin.

APPENDIX 7
Malcolm Baldrige National Quality Program[1]

Core Values and Concepts

The Malcolm Baldrige National Quality Program in Education is based upon 11 core values and concepts:

1. Learning-centered education
2. Leadership
3. Continuous improvement and organizational learning
4. Valuing faculty and staff
5. Partnership development
6. Design quality and prevention
7. Management by fact
8. Long-range view of the future
9. Public responsibility and citizenship
10. Fast response
11. Focus on results

The Seven Baldrige Criteria

There are seven main Criteria for the Malcolm Baldrige National Quality Program. The Criteria are listed below, along with questions adapted from the Baldrige materials. These questions, formulated specially for this third edition of *Schools of Quality,* are designed to help you develop an internal assessment of your school's Quality transformation process and to provide a basic understanding of the scope of the Baldrige program in education.

1. Leadership
How do senior administrators exhibit personal leadership and involvement in creating and sustaining a student focus, clear goals, high expectations, and a leadership system that promotes performance excellence?

---

[1]*Education Criteria for Performance Excellence.* Gaithersburg. Md.: U.S. Department of Commerce. For further information, please contact The Malcolm Baldrige National Quality Program by telephone at (301) 975-2036, or by fax at (301) 948-3716.

---

2. Strategic Planning

How does the school set strategic directions, and how does it determine key plan requirements? How are the plan requirements translated into an effective performance management system, with a primary focus on student performance?

3. Student and Stakeholder Focus

How does the school determine student and stakeholder needs and expectations? How do the levels and trends in key measures of student and stakeholder satisfaction compare with those in comparable schools and organizations?

4. Information and Analysis

How are data and information managed and used effectively to support overall mission-related performance excellence?

5. Faculty and Staff Focus

How are faculty and staff development aligned with the school's performance objectives? How does the school build and maintain a climate conducive to performance excellence, full participation, and personal and organizational growth?

6. Educational and Support Process Management

How are key processes designed, effectively managed, and improved to achieve higher performance in learning-focused education design and delivery, school services, and business operations?

7. School Performance Results

How have improvements been achieved in student performance, in the school's education climate and school services, and in school business operations? How do the school's performance levels compare with those of comparable schools and organizations?

Appendix 8
Sources of Additional Information

BOOKS AND ARTICLES
The Gurus—Their Ideas and Biographies

Deming, W.E. (1986). *Out of the Crisis*. Cambridge, Mass.: MIT Center for Advanced Engineering Study.

The classic work on general principles of continuous improvement through statistical process control. The Deming "bible," including his famous Fourteen Points.

Deming, W.E. (1990). "System of Profound Knowledge." Unpublished monograph.

Explains the four elements that are crucial to the success of any quality journey: appreciation for a system, some knowledge of the theory of variation, a theory of knowledge, and an understanding of human psychology.

Deming, W.E. (1992). *The New Economics for Industry, Education, Government*. Cambridge, Mass.: MIT Center for Advanced Engineering Study.

A further examination of Deming's philosophy and its implications for these three sectors and America's future.

Feigenbaum, A. (1961). *Total Quality Control*. New York: McGraw-Hill.

Industrial applications of Feigenbaum's Total Quality philosophy and practice.

Gabor, A. (1990). *The Man Who Discovered Quality: How W. Edwards Deming Brought the Quality Revolution to America*. New York: Penguin Books.

Detailed biography of Deming by an ardent admirer. Includes detailed accounts of TQM processes at Ford, Xerox, and General Motors.

Ishikawa, K. (1985). *What Is Quality Control? The Japanese Way*. Englewood Cliffs, N.J.: Prentice Hall.

English translation of the late quality expert's introduction to Japanese quality control concepts and procedures, with rather muted references to Deming and Juran.

Juran, J.M. (1988). Juran on Planning for Quality. New York: The Free Press.

An in-depth description of Juran's Quality Trilogy®—quality planning, quality control, and quality improvement, particularly as applied in industry.

Juran, J.M. (1989). *Juran on Leadership for Quality: An Executive Handbook*. New York: The Free Press.

An extension of the concepts and practices detailed in Juran's 1988 work.

Kilian, C. (1992). *The World of W. Edwards Deming*. Knoxville, Tenn.: SPC Press.

An intimate look inside Deming's life and work by his longtime secretary and assistant.

Walton, M. (1991). *Deming Management at Work*. New York: Perigee/Putnam.

Highly readable account of Deming's life and work. Explanations of Deming's Fourteen Points and "seven helpful charts"—otherwise known as the Seven Traditional Tools of TQM.

Walton, M. (1986). *The Deming Management Method*. New York: Perigee/ Putnam.

A brief recap of Deming's teachings, followed by detailed accounts of how his philosophy was applied (successfully) in five instances. Chapter 9, "Lessons Learned," is brief and instructive for all who seek to lead an organizational Quality movement.

Basic TQM Concepts and Practices

Brassard, M. (1989) *The Memory Jogger Plus*. Methuen, Mass.: GOAL/QPC.

A handy little book showing the tools of TQM and examples of how they can be used.

Crosby, P.B. (1980). *Quality Is Free: The Art of Making Quality Certain*. New York: Mentor/Penguin.

Explains that quality, in the long run, is cost-effective because quality is built into every process from the very beginning. "Zero defects" means savings.

Dobyns, L., and C. Crawford-Mason. (1991). *Quality or Else: The Revolution in World Business.* Boston: Houghton Mifflin.

Companion volume for the three-part PBS series. Includes a small section on the well-known Sitka experiment.

Garvin, D.A. (1988). Managing Quality: The Strategic and Competitive Edge. New York: The Free Press.

In-depth look at the quality movement in industry, including the early impact of Deming, Juran, and others on the Japanese "miracle."

Glasser, W. (1994). *The Control Theory Manager.* New York: HarperBusiness.

A brief, superb exploration of Glasser's Control Theory combined with Deming's teachings on Quality Management.

Haberer, J.B., and M.W. Webb. (1994). *TQM: 50 Ways to Make It Work for You.* Menlo Park, Calif.: Crisp Publications.

Fifty essential Quality practices for the effective leader. Includes insightful case studies for personal reflection.

Hunt, V.D. (1992). *Quality in America: How to Implement a Competitive Quality Program.* Homewood, Ill.: Business One Irwin.

One of the most accessible introductions to TQM ideas applied to the improvement of business organizations. Applications to education are easy for readers to draw. Includes self-scoring inventories, tools and techniques of TQM, and a wealth of other information.

Imai, M. (1986). *Kaizen: The Key to Japan's Competitive Success.* New York: McGraw Hill.

Wonderfully readable introduction to the concept of kaizen—the continuous incremental improvement process. Clearly presents applications to schools and other spheres of life.

Lareau, W. (1991). *American Samurai.* New York: Warner.

Twenty "codas" or principles introduce readers to the thinking behind the Quality movement. Although focused on business, educational correlates are rather easy to draw.

Sashkin, M. and K.J. Kiser. (1993). *Putting Total Quality Management to Work.* San Francisco: Berrett-Koehler.

A brief and clearly written introduction to TQM focusing on tools, customers, and culture, with attention to first steps in implementing TQM.

TQM Tools and Techniques

Kume, H. (1985). *Statistical Methods for Quality Improvement.* Tokyo: Association for Overseas Technical Scholarship.

Industrial applications for statistical analysis of quality processes. Advanced reading.

Mizuno, S., ed. (1988). *Management For Quality Improvement.* Cambridge, Mass.: Productivity Press.

Seven "new tools" for TQM application, primarily in industry. Advanced reading.

Ozeki, K., and T. Asaka. (1990). *Handbook of Quality Tools: The Japanese Approach.* Cambridge, Mass.: Productivity Press.

Step-by-step instructions for the use of TQM tools in industry. With a little work, these directions can be interpreted for education.

Scholtes, P.R., et al. (1993). *The Team Handbook for Educators.* Madison, Wis.: Joiner Associates.

How TQM ideas and tools can be used to build effective work teams, and a lot more. This version is adapted from an earlier business-focused work, *The Team Handbook.*

Educational Innovation

Arató, L. (1992). "The World of Work and the World of School: An Interview with John Jay Bonstingl." Original title: "A munka világa es az iskola világa: Interjú J.J. Bonstingl-lel. *Iskolakultúra [School Culture], Journal of the Hungarian Institute of Public Education,* Budapest.

Conversation with the author, conducted by László Arató of the Hungarian Institute of Public Education, on the topic of TQM and its application to schools in their preparation of young people for the global workplace. English translation by Emese Dudás and Erik Csupor, available from The Center for Schools of Quality.

At Home in Our Schools: A Guide to Schoolwide Activities That Build Community. (1994). Oakland, Calif.: Child Development Project.

Practical strategies for bringing parents and community members into your school as supportive partners in the development of young people.

Bailey, E., D.L. Bayless, et al. (N.D.). "The Quality Improvement Management Approach As Implemented in a Middle School." Unpublished manuscript. Rockville, Md.: Westat Inc.

How Deming's Fourteen Points and the Seven Traditional Tools of TQM can help revitalize a middle school.

Berman, L. (1968). *New Priorities in the Curriculum*. Columbus: Charles E. Merrill.

A classic. Particularly interesting is Chapter 1, "Toward Process-Oriented Persons," in which the author urges a "thinking-feeling cohesion" in the development of curriculums and methodologies.

Berman, L., et al. (1991). *Toward Curriculum for Being*. Albany, New York: State University of New York Press.

Transcript of five educators' ongoing dialogue about their own personal and professional journeys—their "curriculum for being."

Bonstingl, J.J. (1996). *Introduction to the Social Sciences*. Fourth edition. Englewood Cliffs, N.J.: Prentice Hall.

Middle school/high school survey course in the seven social sciences, with units on thinking and study skills development. Wrap-up unit focuses on students' options for the future, teaching them how to benefit from S-Teams and several of the new TQM tools described in *Schools of Quality*.

Bonstingl, J.J. (March 1992). "The Total Quality Classroom." *Educational Leadership* 49, 6: 66–70.

Basic ideas of TQM, its history and application to education.

Bonstingl, J.J. (November 1992). "The Quality Revolution in Education." *Educational Leadership* 50, 3: 4–9.

Discusses how the Quality movement is beginning to sweep America, with vignettes of schools here and abroad where Quality principles are being put into practice. The Four Pillars of Quality organizations are described and applied to the work of schools.

Bonstingl, J.J. (January 1993). *Total Quality Management and the Transformation of Education*. Columbia, Md.: The Center for Schools of Quality.

Presentation by the author at the Waseda University International Symposium in Tokyo.

Bonstingl, J.J. (2001). *Schools of Quality.* 3rd ed. Thousand Oaks, Ca.: Corwin Press.

A primer on the Quality Philosophy, its history and application to the continual improvement of education at all levels of functioning.

Borgers, W.F., and T.A., Thompson (1995). *Implementing Continuous Improvement Management in the Schools.* New York: Scholastic.

Lessons learned through the Quality Journey of administrators, staff, and stakeholders in the public schools of Dickinson, Texas.

Bottoms, G., A. Presson, and M. Johnson. (1992). *Making High Schools Work.* Atlanta: Southern Regional Education Board.

An exploration of the factors that contribute to greatest success in high schools, focusing on the integration of academic and vocational education to prepare all young people for competence in the 21st century global workforce.

Brown, G.I., ed. (1975). *The Live Classroom: Innovation Through Confluent Education and Gestalt.* New York: Viking.

An exploration of confluent learning in the classroom-linking students' hearts, heads, and hands to maximize the potentials for learning processes and outcomes.

Brown, R.G. (1991). *Schools of Thought.* San Francisco, Calif.: Jossey-Bass.

Suggests that we create schools where people learn how to be "thoughtful"—in both senses of the term. Particularly useful are the tables at the book's end, guidelines for program review from the Ontario Ministry of Education on issues concerning evaluation of learning processes and outcomes.

Fiske, E.B. (1991). *Smart Schools, Smart Kids: Why Do Some Schools Work?* New York: Simon & Schuster.

A tour of several innovative American schools, with useful insights into the reasons for their successes.

Gardner, H. (1985). *Frames of Mind: The Theory of Multiple Intelligences.* New York: Basic Books.

Gardner's theory of multiple intelligences. Argues that schools have traditionally cultivated a vary narrow spectrum of talents in young people, and proposes remedies.

Glasser, W. (1990). *The Quality School.* New York: Harper & Row.
    Glasser's interpretation of "Choice Theory" as applied to Deming's teachings and school reform.

Glasser, W. (1993). *The Quality School Teacher.* New York: Harper-Perennial.
    A follow-up to *The Quality School,* showing teachers how to implement Deming's Quality Philosophy and Glasser's own Choice Theory in classroom practice.

Goleman, D., P. Kaufman, and M. Ray. (1992). *The Creative Spirit.* New York: Dutton/Penguin.
    Companion volume for the PBS series. Particularly relevant are Chapter 2, "Creativity in Children," and Chapter 4, "Creating Community," which include Howard Gardner's theory of multiple intelligences and a visit to an Italian school where parents are fully involved in the children's joy-filled work at school.

Hansen, B.J., and C.L. Marburger. (1988). *School Based Improvement: A Manual for District Leaders.* Washington, D.C.: National Committee for Citizens in Education.
    Provides ideas for getting everyone involved in your site-based continuous improvement process from the very beginning.

Hansen, B.J., and C.L. Marburger. (1989). *School Based Improvement: A Manual for Training School Councils.* Washington, D.C.: National Committee for Citizens in Education.
    Explains how to train your school governing council for effective interaction and continuous improvement.

Henderson, A. T., C.L. Marburger, and T. Ooms. (1987). *Beyond the Bake Sale: An Educator's Guide to Working With Parents.* Washington, D.C.: National Committee for Citizens in Education.
    Explains how to form positive relationships between educators and parents before a crisis occurs.

Henderson, A.T., and C.L. Marburger. (1990). *A Workbook on Parent Involvement for District Leaders.* Washington, D.C.: National Committee for Citizens in Education.
    Describes ways to build effective parent involvement into school-based improvement.

Hewlett, S.A. (1991). *When the Bough Breaks: The Cost of Neglecting Our Children.* New York: Basic Books.

Provides a wealth of background information on the societal impact of child neglect in America, with the author's proposed action plan for remediation. A glimpse of what happens to some children during the 91 percent of their lives when they are not in school.

An Introduction to Total Quality for Schools. (1991). Arlington, Va.: American Association of School Administrators.

Collection of articles about TQM and its applications to business and education.

The Koalaty Kid Manual. (1991). Milwaukee, Wis.: American Society for Quality.

Presents the basics for schools participating in the Koalaty Kid project.

Kotter, M., and D. Seymour. (1993). *Kidgets.* Milwaukee, Wisc.: American Society for Quality.

A series of insightful vignettes, showing the Quality Philosophy in action within the environment of a school.

Langford, D. (1995). *Orchestrating Student Learning with Quality.* Milwaukee: ASQ Quality Press.

Perspectives on total quality learning processes that grew out of the pioneering experiences of students and staff at Mt. Edgecumbe High School.

McClanahan, E., and C. Wicks. (1994). *Future Force: A Teacher's Handbook for Using TQM in the Classroom.* Glendale, Calif.: Griffin.

Highly practical guide to classroom implementation of the TQM tools. Particularly useful in the elementary and middle school grades.

Marzano, R.J. (1992). *A Different Kind of Classroom: Teaching with Dimensions of Learning.* Alexandria, Va.: Association for Supervision and Curriculum Development.

Introduction to the Dimensions of Learning program, which is useful in creating classroom interaction highly compatible with the TQM philosophy.

Melvin, C.A., III. (Summer 1991). "Restructuring Schools by Applying Deming's Management Theories." *Journal of Staff Development* 12, 3.

A superintendent's view of Deming's teachings and their application to the work of schools.

Neuroth, J., et al. (1992). *TQM Handbook.* Arlington, Va.: American Association of School Administrators.

Applies the Baldrige Award criteria to schools.

Olson, L. (May/June 1992). "Quality is Job One." *Teacher Magazine.*

Discusses how a few schools are applying Deming's teachings. Also in the same issue: "Changing Schools and Classrooms," a synopsis of current reform programs and concepts including cooperative learning, multiple intelligences, and whole language.

Quality Success Stories: Newsletter of the ASCD Quality Education Network.

Inside look at schools and school systems who are putting the Quality Philosophy to work with great success. Includes practical tips for your own Quality journey!

Resource Guide for Total Quality Management in Texas Schools. (1992). Austin, Tex.: Texas Association of School Administrators.

Provides basic information about TQM in education for administrators and teachers.

Rhodes, L.A. (November 1990). "Why Quality Is Within Our Grasp . . . If We Reach." *The School Administrator,* p. 31.

Essential Deming teachings applied to school improvement. Part 1 of a 2-part series.

Rhodes, L.A. (December 1990). "Beyond Your Beliefs: Quantum Leaps Toward Quality Schools." *The School Administrator,* p. 23.

Answers the question: What is "the Deming superintendent" and what does he or she do? Part 2 of a 2-part series.

Rich, D. (1992). *MegaSkills: How Families Help Children Succeed in School and Beyond.* Boston: Houghton Mifflin.

Second edition of a classic about how parents and family members can support their children in schoolwork through greater interaction.

Schargel, F.P. (November/December 1991). "Promoting Quality in Education." *Vocational Education Journal,* p. 34.

Administrator tells how Quality principles were successfully applied at New York City's largest vo-tech school.

Schargel, F.P. (1994). *Transforming Education Through Quality Management.* Princeton, N.J.: Eye On Education.

How Quality practices rejuvenated a Brooklyn vocational high school and energized its students and staff for success.

Schlechty, P.C. (1991). *Schools for the Twenty-First Century: Leadership Imperatives for Educational Reform.* San Francisco, Calif.: Jossey-Bass.

A good analysis of the systemic nature of successful school improvement processes.

Schlechty, P., and B. Cole. (Winter 1991) "Creating a System that Supports Change." *Educational Horizons*, p. 78.

Tells how stakeholders can be helped to create support systems that promote positive change.

Solomon, R.D., N. Davidson, and E.C. Lanter Solomon. (1994). *The Handbook for the Fourth R: Volume III—Relationship Activities for Cooperative and Collegial Learning.* Columbia, Md.: National Institute for Relationship Training, Inc.

An interpersonal relationship training program for professionals.

Stampen, J.O. (1987). "Improving the Quality of Education: W. Edwards Deming and Effective Schools." *Contemporary Education Review* 3, 3: 423.

Examination of linkages between Deming's teachings and effective schools research.

Stanko, J.A. (1991). "A Descriptive Study of the Metodo Natural e Integral as Applied at the Centro de Educacion Natural e Integral Montevideo, Uruguay." Unpublished master's thesis.

An intimate look at how CENI applies continuous improvement and "spiral learning" in this highly successful experimental Uruguayan elementary school.

The State of America's Children Yearbook. Washington, D.C.: Children's Defense Fund.

Annual assessment of conditions facing children in the United States. Of particular interest is the last chapter, which focuses on education.

Total Quality Curriculum. (1993). Leesburg, Virginia: National Vocational Industrial Clubs of America.

Series of modules containing lesson plans and masters designed to teach vocational students how to apply Quality tools and practices to their work.

The Troubled Journey: A Profile of American Youth. (no date). Minneapolis, Minn.: Search Institute.

Booklet detailing the challenges of America's young people (grades 6 through 12), and efforts being made by Search Institute to reverse negative trends by teaching youth how to develop personal character "assets" based upon current strengths.

Wiggins, G. (February 1991). "Standards, Not Standardization: Evoking Quality Student Work." *Educational Leadership* 48, 5: 18–25.

The importance of setting high-quality standards for students to work toward.

Wood, G.H. (1992). *Schools that Work: America's Most Innovative Public Education Programs.* New York: Dutton/Penguin.

Describes schools where community involvement is the key to continuous improvement.

Related Philosophies and Practices

Barker, J.A. (1992). *Future Edge: Discovering the New Paradigms of Success.* New York: William Morrow.

Discusses the significance of paradigms and paradigm shifts in creating contexts for success and improvement.

Beattie, M. (1992). *Gratitude: Affirming the Good Things in Life.* Center City, Minn.: Hazelden Foundation.

Inspiring and practical guide to the daily practice of gratitude, one of the essential disciplines of personal leadership. "Today, I will be grateful. I will start the process of turning today's pain into tomorrow's joy."

Block, P. (1996). *Stewardship: Choosing Service Over Self-Interest.* San Francisco: Berrett-Koehler.

A brilliant exploration of practical strategies for creating a Quality workplace in which all stakeholders are truly enpowered.

Bolman, L.G., and T.E. Deal. (1995). *Leading with Soul: An Uncommon Journey of Spirit.* San Francisco: Jossey-Bass.

An inspiring tale of a leader who discovers, through a painful personal metamorphosis, that true leadership begins with a journey into one's own spirit. He finds that the transformation of his organization must begin with the transformation of his own soul.

Clarke, A.C. (1986). *July 20, 2019: Life in the 21st Century.* New York: Omni/Macmillan.

Science fiction writer's view of daily life in the next century. Chapter 5, "School Days: No Recess," is a compelling look at the gap educators must bridge between past and present realities and the requirements of the future.

Covey, S.R. (1991). *Principle-Centered Leadership.* New York: Summit Books.

Effective leadership is based upon adherence to natural principles and an unwavering focus on total quality and continuous improvement. Chapter 31, "Principle-Centered Learning Environments," applies this concept to schools. Follow-up to his *7 Habits of Highly Effective People.*

Csikszentmihalyi, M. (1990). *Flow, The Psychology of Optimal Experience: Steps Toward Enhancing the Quality of Life.* New York: Harper Perennial.

Improvement of the quality of one's life is inextricably connected with the quality of life in family, community, and work settings. Explains how to optimize the life experience through greater awareness.

De Pree, M. (1989). *Leadership Is an Art.* New York: Doubleday.

Delightful essays on leadership for empowerment by the chairman of Herman Miller, an innovative furniture manufacturing company.

De Pree, M. (1992). *Leadership Jazz.* New York: Doubleday Currency.

More on the topic of humane leadership, development of creativity in workers, and the importance of compassion in all facets of life.

Ferguson, M. (1980). *The Aquarian Conspiracy.* Boston: Houghton Mifflin.

A classic on the art of empowerment in the new paradigm of teaching and learning. Especially compelling is Chapter 9, "Flying and Seeing: New Ways to Learn."

Fromm, E. (1976). *To Have Or To Be?* New York: Harper & Row.

A full treatment of the "having mode" and the "being mode" of existence. Chapter 2, "Having and Being in Daily Experience," applies this philosophy to learning, remembering, reading, and caring.

Kuhn, T. S. (1970). *The Structure of Scientific Revolutions.* Chicago: University of Chicago Press.

The foundation for all subsequent discussions of paradigms and paradigm shifts.

Leonard, G. (1978). *The Silent Pulse.* New York: E.P. Dutton.

Intriguing exploration of the ways humans are intrinsically connected within their own selves and with other humans.

Lewin, K. (1948). *Resolving Social Conflicts.* New York: Harper.

The Force Field, now widely used as a TQM tool, was first developed in this work.

McCarthy, K.W. (1992). *The On-Purpose Person: Making Your Life Make Sense.* Colorado Springs, Colo.: Piñon Press.

An inspirational allegory of a person who discovers that living with a clear focus on his key purposes is the best route to a high-quality life.

Marshall, R., and M. Tucker. (1992). *Thinking for a Living: Work, Skills, and the Future of the American Economy.* New York: Basic Books.

American education today reflects the factory model of the Industrial Revolution. The authors describe the changes necessary if schools are to prepare young people for the global working world of the future.

Nair, K. (1990). *Beyond Winning: The Handbook for the Leadership Revolution.* Phoenix: Paradox Press.

Essential principles for building partnership environments.

Orsborn, C. (1992). *Inner Excellence.* San Rafael, Calif.: New World Library.

Seven principles for reclaiming quality in your personal and professional life.

Rogers, C. (1980). *A Way of Being.* Boston: Houghton Mifflin.

How to build person-centered communities, schools, and businesses. "The Process of Education and Its Future" speaks to the need for heartful schools if we are serious about maximizing the potentials of young people.

Sashkin, M., and R.L. Williams. (1990). "Does Fairness Make a Difference?" *Organizational Dynamics*, 19, 2, pp. 56-71.

Research shows that workers' perceptions of 9 aspects of fairness in the workplace impact directly the organization's productivity, absentee rates, and the physical and mental health of employees.

Schlossstein, (1989). *The End of the American Century*. New York: Congdon and Weed.

Explores what went wrong with America and how we can make it right. Part 3, "The Legacy of Confucius: Forging Educational Excellence," sheds light on social and educational issues from a multinational perspective.

Von Oech, R. (1983). *A Whack on the Side of the Head*. New York: Warner Books.

A highly entertaining workbook for those who want to explore their own creative capabilities beyond the "one right answer." Tells how to open the 10 "mental locks" blocking your natural creativity.

Von Oech, R. (1986). *A Kick in the Seat of the Pants*. New York: Perennial Library/Harper & Row.

Another entertaining workbook on developing creativity in yourself and others through the "four roles of the creative process: the explorer, the artist, the judge, and the warrior."

Wellins, R.S., W.C. Byham, and J.M. Wilson. (1991). *Empowered Teams: Creating Self-Directed Work Groups That Improve Quality, Productivity, and Participation*. San Francisco, Calif.: Jossey-Bass.

Explains how to build strong, interactive, effective teams from the ground up.

Business Perspectives

Altany, D. (November 5, 1990). "Copycats." *Industry Week*, pg. 11.

A good introduction to the use of benchmarking in businesses' continuous improvement processes. Copying isn't cheating anymore!

America's Choice: High Skills or Low Wages! (1990). Rochester, New York: National Center on Education and the Economy.

Landmark document citing an action plan for business and education to use to improve the workforce of tomorrow.

Block, P. (1991) . *The Empowered Manager: Positive Political Skills at Work*. San Francisco, Calif.: Jossey-Bass.

A warm and insightful look at how managers can best empower themselves and all other people in the organization.

Blueprint for Business on Restructuring Education. (1989). Washington, D.C.: National Alliance of Business.

A guidebook for businesses to build "comfort zones" and mutual support projects with schools.

Bowles, J., and J. Hammond. (1991). *Beyond Quality: How 50 Winning Companies Use Continuous Improvement*. New York: G.P. Putnam's Sons.

The title says it all. Its three appendixes summarize the Baldrige Award criteria, the ideas of the TQM pioneers, and the guidelines for a national government quality award.

Bradford, D.L., and A.R. Cohen. (1984). *Managing for Excellence: The Guide to Developing High Performance in Contemporary Organizations*. New York: John Wiley and Sons.

Explains how managers can develop a successful learning organization through team-building.

Cheales, P. (1994). *The "I was your Customer" Workbook: The Survival Kit for World-Class Customer Delight*. Rivonia, South Africa: William Waterman Publications.

Slim volume of good insights into the fine art of discerning customer needs before your customers are aware of those needs. Written from the perspective of a customer.

Glasser, W. (1994). *The Control Theory Manager*. New York: HarperBusiness.

An exploration of the benefits of lead-management, in which the author combines the Quality Philosophy with his own Control Theory.

Halberstam, D. (1986). *The Reckoning*. New York: William Morrow.

Extensive history of American automobile industry's rise, fall, and attempted resurrection. Especially interesting: Chapter 17, "Deming Finds An Audience"—an account of Deming's early work with Japan's carmakers.

Howard, V.A., and J.H. Barton. (1992). *Thinking Together: Making Meetings Work.* New York: William Morrow.

Designed for companies, these insights are equally valuable for educators who want to use their limited time together most productively.

Johnson, W.B., and A.E. Packer. (1987). *Workforce 2000: Work and Workers for the Twenty-First Century.* Indianapolis: Hudson Institute.

Essential data for understanding America's shifting demographics and what they mean for education.

Jones, P., and L. Kahaner. (1995). *Say It and Live It: The 50 Corporate Mission Statements That Hit the Mark.* New York: Currency Doubleday.

Insightful look at outstanding mission statements and the world-class companies that created them. A great benchmarking resource for educators.

Kolberg, W.H., and F.C. Smith. (1992). *Rebuilding America's Workforce.* Homewood, Ill.: Business One Irwin.

Detailed examination of America's declining productivity with prescriptions for educators, families, businesses, and communities. See especially Chapter 8: "Closing the Education Gap."

Learning a Living: A Blueprint for High Performance—A SCANS Report for America 2000. (1992). Washington, D.C.: U.S. Department of Labor.

Follow-up to *What Work Requires of Schools.* Explains the basic workplace skills young people should have for success.

Lynch, R.F. (April 1991). "Shedding the Shackles of George Patton, Henry Ford, and First-Grade Teachers." *Quality Progress*, p. 63.

What American education must consider in examining Taylorism.

Nykiel, R.A. (1992). *You Can't Lose If the Customer Wins.* Stamford, Conn.: Longmeadow Press.

A primer on customer-supplier relations and business success.

Ohmae, K. (1990). *The Borderless World: Power and Strategy in the Interlinked Economy.* New York: Harper Business.

A look at the importance of quality in the global marketplace.

O'Toole, J. (1993). *The Executive's Compass: Business and the Good Society.* New York: Oxford University Press.

A timely exploration of the role business leaders must play in the development of a Quality-focused society.

Petersen, D.E., and J. Hillkirk. (1991). *A Better Idea: Redefining the Way Americans Work.* Boston: Houghton Mifflin.

How Ford Motor Company turned itself around, making quality every employee's "Job 1."

Roddick, A. (1991). *Body and Soul: Profits with Principles.* New York: Crown Publishers.

The key to success is for company management to establish environments in which workers' creativity is unleashed and their potentials are maximized. By the founder of the Body Shop chain of stores.

Rosenbluth, H.F., and D.M. Peters. (1992). *The Customer Comes Second.* New York: William Morrow.

Who comes first? Your workers do! The way you treat your workers is the way they treat customers. Implications for school administrators?

Sanders, B. (1995). *Fabled Service: Ordinary Acts, Extraordinary Outcomes.* San Diego: Pfeiffer & Company.

A leader's guide to Quality service. Inside looks at Nordstrom, Scandinavian Air System, ServiceMaster, Marriott, and other high-quality service-focused organizations. "Fabled service is inseparable from integrity," the author observes.

Senge, P.M. (1990). *The Fifth Discipline: The Art and Practice of the Learning Organization.* New York: Doubleday Currency.

Businesses and other organizations must become "learning organizations" that promote learning if they are to survive and thrive.

Senge, P.M. (Fall 1990). "The Leader's New Work: Building Learning Organizations." *Sloan Management Review* 31, 1: 7.

A good synthesis of *The Fifth Discipline*.

Senge, P.M. (1994). *The Fifth Discipline Fieldbook: Strategies and Tools for Building a Learning Organization.* New York: Doubleday Currency.

Highly practical applications of the Fifth Discipline theory to the daily practice of effective leadership. Dozens of wonderful insights, strategies, and tools easily adapted for organizational change in schools.

Townshend, P.L., and J.E. Gebhardt. (1990). *Commit To Quality.* New York: John Wiley and Sons.

How the author, as CEO of an innovative insurance company, "talks the walk and walks the talk" of quality.

Townshend, P.L., and J.E. Gebhardt. (1992). *Quality in Action: 93 Lessons in Leadership, Participation, and Measurement*. New York: John Wiley and Sons.

A wealth of insights into the creation and growth of quality organizations, with a few ideas specifically for education.

What Work Requires of Schools: A SCANS Report for America 2000. (1991). Washington, D.C.: U.S. Department of Labor.

Presents the basic competencies required of today's workers by business, with implications for schools, families, and communities.

AUDIO AND VIDEO MATERIALS

Assignment: Total Quality Management For Schools. (1992). Columbia, Md.: The Center for Schools of Quality.

Audiotape conversation with John Jay Bonstingl, focusing on how his Four Pillars of Schools of Quality and Deming's Fourteen Points can reinvigorate schools, as they have done for many businesses.

Creating Schools of Quality: The New Work of School Administrators, Staff Developers, and Policy Makers. (1994). Alexandria, Va.: ASCD.

A 90-minute audiocassette of a special session by John Jay Bonstingl at the 1994 ASCD Annual Conference in Chicago.

Educational Leadership on Tape. (November 1992). Alexandria, Va.: ASCD.

Audiotape renditions of articles in the journal's November 1992 issue, which focuses on TQM in education.

Discovering the Future: The Business of Paradigms. (1989). Burnsville, Minn.: Charthouse Learning Corporation.

Joel Barker introduces the concept of paradigms and illustrates their significance in preparing for change. Videotape and 16mm formats.

Discovering the Future: The Power of Vision. (1990). Burnsville, Minn.: Charthouse Learning Corporation.

Joel Barker explores the relationship between positive visions of the future and the development of creativity in individuals and organizations. Videotape and 16mm film formats.

If Japan Can, Why Can't We? (1980). Chicago: Films, Inc.

The original NBC TV documentary that introduced America to the work of Deming in Japan.

Koalaty Kid: A Commitment to Quality in Elementary Education. (1992). Milwaukee, Wis.: ASQ.

Eight-minute videotape overview of the Koalaty Kid project in action at Carder Elementary School in Corning, New York.

Principle-Centered Leadership. (1991). Provo, Utah: Covey Leadership Center.

Audiotape adaptation by Stephen Covey of the material in his book of the same title. Six-tape set.

Quality Or Else! (1991). Chicago: Films, Inc.

Three-part PBS series on the TQM revolution in business and education, and why it is desperately needed. Videotape format.

Quest for Excellence. (Annual). Milwaukee, Wisc.: American Society for Quality.

Superbly produced video, giving the viewer an inside look at the companies who have won the annual Malcolm Baldrige National Quality Award. A great educator's resource for benchmarking.

Quest for Quality. (1991). Arlington, Va.: American Association of School Administrators.

Interviews with John Jay Bonstingl, Stephen Covey, William Glasser, David Langford, and others on the topic of TQM applied to the work of schools. Two audiotapes.

Schools of Quality. (1994). Alexandria, Va.: ASCD.

Award-winning companion video to the Corwin book *Schools of Quality.* Three school sites show how they use Bonstingl's Four Pillars of Quality at every level of functioning.

Schools of Quality: Creating Success for All. (March 1993). Columbia, Maryland: The Center for Schools of Quality.

Audiotape of a keynote address by John Jay Bonstingl at an international education conference in Nairobi, Kenya.

Total Quality at Prairie View Elementary: A New Way of Learning. (1995). Cedar Rapids, Iowa: Woods Quality Center.

Video tour of a Quality-Focused school in which students and teachers use the Quality philosophy and tools to plan, complete, and assess their work together.

W. Edwards Deming: Prophet of Quality. (1992) Chicago: Films, Inc.
The life and work of Deming. Videotape format.

The Deming Library. Chicago: Films, Inc.
A 16-part videotape series in which W. Edwards Deming explains and demonstrates his philosophy.

ORGANIZATIONS AND NETWORKS

Baldrige National Quality Program
Contact: Harry Hertz
Director
Route 270 and Quince Orchard Rd.
Administration Bldg., Rm. A537
Gaithersburg, MD 20899
(301) 975-2036
Directs the Malcolm Baldrige National Quality Program, which invites schools, school systems, and other educational organizations to apply the seven Baldrige criteria to their functioning at all levels.

Search Institute
Contact: Peter L. Benson
President
700 S. Third St., Suite 210
Minneapolis, MN 55415
(612) 376-8955
Nonprofit organization dedicated to helping educators build 30 essential character "assets" in young people. Conducts highly effective school-and-community climate assessments as part of this work.

Quality Education Network of the Association for Supervision and
    Curriculum Development
Contact: John Jay Bonstingl
Facilitator
c/o The Center for Schools of Quality
P.O. Box 810
Columbia, MD 21044
(410) 997-7555
Grassroots network to share and learn about Quality practices in education. Newsletter, membership list, and advance notice about conferences, seminars, and materials on quality in schools.

AASA Quality Network
4401 6th Street, S.W.
Cedar Rapids, IA 52404
(319) 399-6465
   Newsletter, Quality-focused articles, information about conferences, seminars, and products.

American Society for Quality
Contact: Suzanne Keely
Manager, Koalaty Kid Program
P.O. Box 3005
Milwaukee, WI 53201
(800) 248-1946 outside Milwaukee
   Membership organization of statistical quality control professionals. Institutional home of the worldwide Koalaty Kid project. Information, videotape about the project. Membership in ASQ includes *Quality Progress,* a monthly publication about quality issues.

The Center for Schools of Quality
Contact: John Jay Bonstingl
Director
P.O. Box 810
Columbia, MD 21044
(410) 997-7555
   Instructional materials and training for school leaders, policymakers, teachers, parents, businesses, and communities, focusing on the application of Quality principles and practices.

GOAL/QPC
Contact: Bob King
Chief Executive Officer
2 Manor Parkway
Salem, New Hampshire 03079
(800) 207-5813 or (603) 893-1944
   Nonprofit Quality research and publishing organization.

Home and School Institute, Inc.
Contact: Dorothy Rich
President
1201 Sixteenth Street, N. W.
Washington, DC 20036
(202) 466-3633

Innovative programs for families and teachers working together to nurture children's achievement in the school, at home, and in the community.

National Institute for Relationship Training, Inc.
Contact: Richard D. Solomon
President
9240 Broken Timber Way
Columbia, MD 21045
(410) 730-5500

Instructional materials and training for educators and students in active listening, team-building, and other essential skills.

Woods Quality Center
Contact: Robert "Mick" McNiel
Director
4401 6th St., S.W.
Cedar Rapids, IA 52404
(319) 399-6465

Producer and distributor of Quality-focused material for educators who wish to apply the Quality philosophy in their schools.

References

Ackoff, R. (1993). *Ackoff's Fables.* New York: John Wiley & Sons, p. xii.

Barker, J.A. (1992). *Future Edge.* New York: Morrow, p. 31.

Bayless, D.L., G. Massaro, et. al. (1992). "SouthEastern Regional Vision for Education: Quality Improvement." Unpublished document, p. 80.

Berman, L.M. (1968). *New Priorities in the Curriculum.* Columbus: Merrill, p. 9.

Bonstingl, J.J. (1991). *Introduction to the Social Sciences.* Englewood Cliffs, N.J.: Prentice Hall.

Bonstingl, J.J. (March 1992). "The Total Quality Classroom." *Educational Leadership* 49, 6: 67.

Brown, G.I. (1975). *The Live Classroom: Innovation Through Confluent Education and Gestalt.* New York: The Viking Press.

Clarke, A.C. (1986). *July 20, 2019: Life in the 21st Century.* New York: Omni/Macmillan, p. 76.

Crosby, P. (1980). *Quality Is Free: The Art of Making Quality Certain.* New York: Mentor/Penguin.

Deming, W.E. (1986). *Out of the Crisis.* Cambridge, Mass.: MIT Center for Advanced Engineering Study.

Deming, W.E. (1990). "System of Profound Knowledge." Unpublished monograph.

Deming, W.E. (January 23–24), 1992. Seminar.

Ferguson, M. (1980). *The Aquarian Conspiracy.* Los Angeles, Calif.: Tarcher, p. 228.

Fromm, E. (1976). *To Have Or To Be?* New York: Harper & Row, p. 29, 77–78.

Gabor, A. (1990). *The Man Who Discovered Quality.* New York: Penguin, p. 77.

Garvin, D.A. (1988). *Managing Quality.* New York: The Free Press, pp. 180–184.

Glasser, W. (1992). *The Quality School: Managing Students Without Coercion.* New York: HarperPerennial.

Gottlieb, D. (January 15, 1984). *The Washington Post*, page D-3.

Halberstam, D. (1986). *The Reckoning.* New York: Morrow, p. 314–315.

Henderson, A.T., C.L. Marburger, and T. Ooms. (1987). *Beyond the Bake Sale: An Educator's Guide to Working with Parents.* Washington, D.C.: National Committee for Citizens in Education.

Ishikawa, K. (1985). *What Is Total Quality Control? The Japanese Way.* Englewood Cliffs, N.J.: Prentice Hall, pp. 25–29.

Juran, J.M. (1988). *Juran on Planning for Quality.* New York: The Free Press, pp. 6–15.

Kilian, C. (1992). *The World of W. Edwards Deming.* Knoxville, Tennessee: SPC Press, p. 174.

Koalaty Kid Manual. (1991). Milwaukee, Wisc.: American Society for Quality Control, p. ii.

Leonard, G. (1978). *The Silent Pulse.* New York: Dutton, p. 41.

Lewin, K. (1948). *Resolving Social Conflicts.* New York: Harper.

Lynch, R.F. (April 1991). "Shedding the Shackles of George Patton, Henry Ford, and First-Grade Teachers." *Quality Progress,* p. 64.

Marshall, R. and M. Tucker. (1992) *Thinking for a Living: Work, Skills, and the Future of the American Economy.* New York: Basic Books, p. 17.

The Quality Revolution. (1989). Film broadcast on PBS, Dystar Television.

Sashkin, M., and K.J. Kiser. (1993) *Putting Total Quality Management to Work.* San Francisco, Calif.: Berrett-Koehler Publishers, pp. 4–5.

Senge, P.M. (1990). *The Fifth Discipline.* New York: Doubleday, p. 4.

Scholtes, P.R. (1988). *The Team Handbook.* Madison, Wisc.: Joiner Associates, pp. 2-18 to 2-21.

Stanko, J.A. (1988). "A Descriptive Study of the Metodo Natural e Integral as Applied at the Centro de Educacion Natural e Integral Montevideo, Uruguay." Unpublished Master's thesis, p. 68.

Taba, H., et al. (1971). *A Teacher's Handbook to Elementary Social Studies: An Inductive Approach.* Reading, Mass.: Addison-Wesley.

von Oech, R. (1983). *A Whack on the Side of the Head.* New York: Warner, p. 21.

Walton, M. (1986). *The Deming Management Method.* New York: Perigee/Putnam, p. 13.

Walton, M. (1991). *Deming Management at Work.* New York: Perigee/Putnam, p. 16.

Praise for *Schools of Quality*, Third Edition

"The quality journey requires a commitment on both the personal and the institutional level. Bonstingl's Five Practices of Quality are the essential building blocks to attain personal goals that will lead to the attainment of institutional excellence. He is truly a leader of the Quality revolution."

Linda James, Ph.D.
Emeritus Examiner, Malcolm Baldrige National Quality Award

*"Jay Bonstingl has become one of the most well-known writers within the borders of Turkey as a result of **Schools of Quality**. The reason it's one of the best-sellers within the field is Bonstingl's style and approach and the samples from the real world and the school environment. Turkish teachers and principals consider themselves lucky to have such a book!*

Hayal Köksal
Co-Founder, Turkish Center for Schools of Quality
Istanbul

*"My hat's off to Jay Bonstingl and his third edition of **Schools of Quality** for pointing out that 'quality in schools' is a process of working in teams, self-assessment, improvement of systems, and having students actively engaged in their learning through problem solving tools and the use of data for continuous improvement."*

Mick McNiel
Director
National Quality Network of the American
Association of School Administrators
Cedar Rapids, Iowa

*"**Schools of Quality** is a must read for every educator. Jay Bonstingl writes a persuasive prescription for keeping schools healthy and alive.*

Anthony Scannella, Ed.D.
Director of Professional Development
Foundation for Educational Administration
Jamesburg, New Jersey

"A reader-friendly book filled with essential wisdom to help educators grow Quality in the lives of their students and make Quality a way of being in their own personal and professional lives."

Louise Voss Thurn
School Improvement Facilitator
Keystone Area Education Agency
Elkader, Iowa

**CORWIN
PRESS**

The Corwin Press logo—a raven striding across an open book—represents the happy union of courage and learning. We are a professional-level publisher of books and journals for K–12 educators, and we are committed to creating and providing resources that embody these qualities. Corwin's motto is "Success for All Learners."